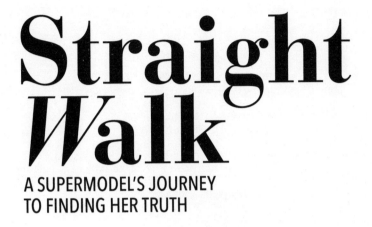

Straight *Walk*

A SUPERMODEL'S JOURNEY
TO FINDING HER TRUTH

A MEMOIR

PATRICIA VELASQUEZ

Published by Post Hill Press
109 International Drive, Suite 300
Franklin, TN 37067

To my mother, Lidela
To my daughter, Maya

Some names have been changed to protect people's identities.

Prologue

The pain of telling a lie cut deep. Each time I told one, however small it seemed, it tore its way into every fiber of my being. But *living* a lie year after year, that was particularly torturous, and the longer I lived it the more I realized that the lie, that pretend life I'd created and the real one I had pretended didn't exist, was eroding my soul bit by bit, absorbing into the crevices of who I once was. It burdened everything I did, every thought I had. Physically, I was there—wherever I needed to be at the time—but spiritually and mentally, living a lie isolated me, made me feel like more of an outsider than I already felt on most days, and it created loneliness and self-loathing so overwhelming that it bled through my pores. All the fame, success, and celebrity on the planet couldn't wash away the damage.

I thought lying was saving my family from pain when in fact it was inflicting constant unspoken pain on them and preventing them from growing and walking their own walk. I thought I was lying *for* them. Or I was simply lying to myself to stop my own pain; maybe I had convinced myself that what I was doing was best for them. It wasn't good for any of us, and I learned far too late the implications my secret would have on my life and, worst of all, on those I loved most in the world.

Part One

Chapter One

My first lie came easily to me.

Limayri and I were getting bumped and pushed as we stood elbow to elbow with fifteen thousand other anxious teenagers waiting in a penned-off area for the gates to open, excited to enter the concert. We lived in one of the hottest cities not just in Venezuela, but on the entire planet. And the humidity that day was oppressive. Sweat dripped from our foreheads and down our backs, and down the back of my legs, which always sweat. I hadn't even wanted to come, but my sister had begged me earlier that week to join her.

"Patricia, they are the biggest band in the world right now," she pleaded one night in our bedroom in our apartment. "Please."

"I love them, but I don't want to go stand there and scream at a band," I said.

"But Mamá said if you come with me, I can go." Limayri was seventeen and I was fifteen. I knew she really wanted to be there, so I relented and agreed to go with her.

As I waited for the gates to Plaza de Toros, the bullfighting stadium turned concert hall, to open, I suddenly *did* want to scream, surprised at how caught up I was in the frenzy for this famous Spanish band that had made its way to my city, Maracaibo. The crazy energy surrounded us. When they finally opened the gates, hundreds of teenagers with floor tickets rushed in like a dam breaking, and my sister and I ran as fast as we could to get to the front row. There were no seats where we were, nothing assigned. It was standing room only in the dirt where the bulls would normally run and fight. We bolted faster than everyone, running like bulls ourselves, and we made our way right up to the stage.

The crowd was enormous—and loud. Everyone exuded such happiness, especially Limayri, who was wearing super-tight jeans. She liked tight clothing, and it always looked great on her. We had edged our way as close as possible to where the musicians would be—we were right there. Everyone was screaming, the sound of anxious teens almost deafening, and in what felt like minutes, the lights dimmed, the stage lit up, and the band stepped out and started singing music like we'd never heard. They were cutting edge and ahead of their time, performing a soulful take on pop.

I barely noticed the lead singer, a petite woman, or the drummer and two others, but I was struck by the bass player off to the side, in his rugged brown leather jacket, despite the heat, and jeans. Mega-struck. I couldn't take my eyes off him. He was so attractive with his short, curly brown hair and kind of big nose. He smiled to the side. I liked the way he moved—the way he tapped his foot to the rhythm of the bass. Almost as soon as the band started playing, I weirdly fell for him. Like, madly. I suddenly had an instant crush on this man I didn't even know. I felt a physical sensation in my stomach and in my heart, which was pounding. I think I was a little bit starstruck as well because I had never really seen a band this famous, and had certainly never been so close to celebrity. I had been to concerts before, but this was the biggest.

As I stared at him, he started looking back at me. I didn't break our gaze, though he looked down at times as he played. I laughed when I heard the girl next to me talking.

"Oh my God," she said. "He's looking at me." She was yelling it to anyone who would listen. "He's looking at me."

She was talking about my guy. Every time she said it, which was often, I smiled. But I knew he was looking at me, not this stranger to my left. But everyone was crazy for this band, so it's not like I didn't understand how amazing it would feel for anyone to receive the attention directed at me.

I looked away from him for a second, abruptly distracted as I witnessed a girl fainting at the end of my row. She fell to the ground with a thud. The heat and the excitement were too much for her, it seemed. Within seconds, a big, beefy, bald security guard in a black T-shirt and jeans, his arms covered in tattoos, rushed out and scooped her up, bringing her off to the side of the stage for help. Over the next hour as the band played, several girls dropped to the ground just as that one had.

As a slower song began to fade and a crazy, jump-to-your-feet one began, I realized the concert was coming to an end. They were going out with a bang, and the entire stadium was screaming and jumping, knowing that things were wrapping up. I started to feel a little desperate. I needed to get to this musician I'd been so taken with.

Without taking my eyes off him, I leaned over to Limayri, yelling over the music but hoping no one else would hear me. "Hold my hand," I said as I grabbed her hand. Darkness had set in. The sky was pitch black.

She didn't ask why; she just held on. Then I let my knees buckle beneath me, and I fell to the dirt with my eyes closed. I didn't wear tight jeans; instead, I used my brother Carlo's hand-me-downs. They were baggy and comfortable for me as I fell, not constricting. Limayri hung on for dear life, and within seconds I was seized by a guard and, with Limayri running beside me, carried backstage.

I didn't open my eyes until I could tell by the noise that we were away from the crowds. I could hear the music, but the screaming fans were far away. I finally opened my eyes and looked at my sister beside me.

"Are you okay?" Her eyes were wide open and starting to fill with tears. I knew she was scared. I should have told her ahead of time that I had planned to faint on purpose, but I knew it had been too loud to explain and I needed to act quickly.

I looked around and knew instantly that I was backstage. I could see the steps leading up to the stage where the band was still playing. They would soon walk right by us.

The guard put me on the steps for a few seconds. When I stood up, I made sure I was wobbly-looking. I caught Limayri's eye and gave her a wink. She knew immediately that I had just gotten us backstage. Sharp as always, she gave me a modest nod and then played right along.

"Oh my God," I said. They brought me a chair and I sat back down.

"I'm so glad you're okay!" Limayri said. "You're okay, right?" She put her hand on my forehead. "Oh, Patricia, you're still hot. Oh no. Are you sick?" She was good. She gave me a knowing look, and I could tell she was holding back a smile. This made her day even more than she could have imagined when we left home that afternoon. To be backstage—not just front row—was an entirely new level of bragging rights for her.

A few seconds later the music ended and the stage lights darkened. I heard the fans screaming in the distance. I looked toward the stage, and the musicians came barreling down the stairs, the sound of their boots clanking loudly on the metal steps as they moved. My guy was the third one to exit the stage, and before he had even gotten close to the steps, he made eye contact with me. I realized he had seen me faint and probably knew I'd be there when he exited.

He came downstage and stopped in front of me. Limayri was just staring at this point, shocked and smiling. The last few musicians jumped down the stairs, and one smacked my guy on the back as he walked by.

"Hi," he said. "What's your name?"

I panicked a little. I didn't know whether to stand up again or if that would give away that I had pretended to fall. I remained seated and said, "Patricia."

"I'm Ernesto," he said.

I turned to Limayri and said frantically, "Do you have paper?" She looked stunned and didn't move. "Quick," I said. "Paper!" Backstage felt frenzied. Everyone was hustling, and the band was racing out. Workers were already breaking down some of the stuff onstage.

My sister reached into her bag, pulled out her concert ticket, and handed it to me. I pulled a pen out of my bag and wrote down the phone number for our apartment. I handed it to him without saying anything. I knew I had very little time to make my move.

"You're okay?" he asked.

"Yes. I had to be closer to you," I said, surprised I'd given myself up so easily. "Call me." I handed him our number at home.

"Okay," he said. "We're leaving first thing in the morning for Caracas, though. But I will call you."

I knew he probably had many girls doing what I had just done and that he was used to this kind of thing, but I felt a sense of sincerity from him. His voice was soft, his eyes authentic. He looked me right in the eyes and smiled. He put my number in his front jeans pocket, touched my shoulder, and left.

That night, back at home in our apartment, I stayed awake staring at the white walls, almost hypnotized by them. All night long, I sat out in the living room waiting for him to call, a bit worried my mother would notice that I was up to something. There was a phone in the kitchen and one in her room, so I had to stay as close as possible so she wouldn't answer it before I did. I couldn't sleep—not that I wanted to. I needed to hear his voice. All I could think is, *He's going to call. He's going to call. He's going to call.*

He didn't. The phone never rang that night. I wondered as I sat if I'd given him the wrong number or if he'd lost the paper. I had been so certain I'd hear from him. The next morning I didn't go to school. I couldn't. I had to wait. I told my mother I was sick, and because I was never sick, she believed me. I had never given her any reason to think I was telling anything but the truth. Limayri was the free spirit, not me. I was a straight shooter. She was fun and spontaneous. I followed the rules more, colored inside the lines. And I'd certainly never lied to my mother.

My brothers, sisters, and mother left that morning for school and work. Once everyone was gone, I panicked. I felt like I had to see him. I was so obsessed that it didn't matter what happened; I had to see this man. I just had to. By mid-afternoon, the phone still hadn't rung and I was trying to figure out how to track down this musician. I decided that if he didn't call me, I'd find his number and call him myself.

I walked into the kitchen, opened a drawer, and pulled out a phone book. He had said he was leaving that day, and leaving meant the capital. I flipped through the yellow pages and made a list of all the nice five-star hotels in Caracas, and one by one started calling them looking for my rock star. By the fourth hotel I got lucky.

"Hilton Hotel, how may I direct your call?" a receptionist said.

"Ernesto Escudero's room, please," I said, gripping the phone receiver tightly. I had called a friend at school early that morning to help me figure out his last name.

"Hold one second," the voice said.

I gasped. I couldn't believe I had found this man. I waited in silence with the receiver to my ear.

"He's not picking up in his room. May I take a message?" the receptionist asked when she returned to the line.

My head was spinning. Without thinking about it I said, "It is urgent that you give this message to him. It's a matter of life and death. I know he will be leaving very soon, and this is a family matter, so please have him call me right away." I gave her all my information.

"Don't worry. I'll make sure he gets the message," she said. We hung up.

I hadn't even changed out of my pajamas yet, and I wasn't about to. I needed to continue waiting by the phone. My sisters and brothers would eventually come home from school, and my mom from work. I knew he was going to call me back. I thought perhaps he was at rehearsal for a concert later that night. What else could he be doing that would prevent him from calling me? I figured he'd be back soon. All this was swirling in my head as I sat perched on a chair in the kitchen, hugging my knees so that my feet rested on the seat too.

The door opened and my younger sister, Caty, came in. Her uniform always looked as pristine and pressed at the end of the day as it did when she left in the morning. She gave me a glance, knew I was up to something, and walked straight past me into her room, always great at minding her own business. I watched her walk by, momentarily forgetting my mission, when suddenly I was startled back to it with the ring of the phone. I grabbed it before the first ring even finished. I knew it was him and I knew I was about to do something crazy.

That phone call changed my life. At the time, I had no idea to what extent.

Chapter Two

We lived on the fifteenth floor in an area called Valle Frio. I used to stand out on the balcony and cover the bottom of my face with my hand, so the only view I could see as I stared out was a beautiful one—seeing only the really good neighborhood that ran along the edge of the lake, deep in the distance. My mom would often sit in the living room on her rocking chair and watch westerns. She loved cowboy movies. But seeing them and the dry land the horses ran around on, which looked like a desert to me, actually gave me this overwhelming feeling of thirst. So when the TV went on, I'd go stand on the balcony after a few minutes and block out everything but the lake and the sailboats, dreaming of being out there with those people, on the water, in the water.

When I was just a year old, we left our then new apartment in Venezuela because my dad was offered an academic post and work with UNESCO in Paris. I don't remember much at all about those years, but I was told I started speaking French around the same time I started speaking Spanish. From Paris, a few years later, we moved to Pátzcuaro, Mexico, for another post with UNESCO, living in a beautiful enclosed community with a giant park in the middle, where we ran freely, climbing trees and playing. I remember it had the most enormous Mexican-looking fountain—with tile and red clay—in front of the main house. It was a fun place to live.

Eventually we moved back to Maracaibo into the apartment we'd bought on the hill less than a decade earlier, but everything there had dramatically changed for the worse. It was what we called an invasion. A building was built and then, as the years went by, it became surrounded by huts and extreme poverty. A barrio emerged. Our apartment inside remained impeccable and beautiful, thanks to my mother's tireless efforts to make a nice home for us. But, below my hand as I looked out from my balcony, when I moved it away to see the full view, that was my reality. Poverty surrounded our once shining new building, which was now in need of repair in every corner. The immediate surrounding neighborhood looked like a desert too—dry and decrepit, void of vibrancy and greenery. It hadn't been a poor part of town years and years ago. When my family bought the apartment, just before I was born, it was the only building around at the time—modern and new in what was expected to be an up-and-coming place. But by the time we returned, our building was surrounded by favelas and huts—some made poorly with concrete, some with metal roofs. It was true poverty. Our building was suddenly in a very poor part of town, but misplaced.

My mother did her best to give us all a great life. Sundays were something special because we'd pile into the car, get out of our neighborhood, and go to the water with our extended family. We were, after all, a Caribbean country. We'd drive to a beach called Caimare Chico in the Wayuu region, which was safe back then, though that changed in later years. My mother had eleven brothers and sisters. I had more than one hundred first cousins, so when a lot of us went, it was a large gathering. The kids would swim all day, and there'd be music blaring, beer to drink, and sheep on the grill. The beach was packed with tons of families having fun just like ours, and the one road in and out was always filled with car accidents because people would get drunk and drive home. It was a crazy but wonderful place. My aunts would sit under umbrellas or under these straw huts on the sand and gossip. My mom was allergic to the sun, so she'd stay in the shade, though every once in a while she'd step out, walk to the water, and put just her feet in. She'd kneel down and splash a little onto her arms and face, never venturing too far in, and then she'd go back to the hut. I assumed she couldn't swim but wondered why she never went in a bit farther.

I always felt the love, but we weren't outwardly affectionate people. There was no hugging or saying "I love you," because Wayuu people aren't expressive by nature. But love to me meant commitment and sacrifice, as exemplified by my mother's work to keep us happy and healthy. My mother worked as the director of a kindergarten with eight hundred children. It was a huge responsibility because it was the largest school in the state, but she managed it well. Every day she would come home from work and take care of us all, alone basically. She never complained and did her best to make us feel like we had enough, but looking back, the pressure must have been immense for her. Because she was a shy and quiet woman, she never complained and we never talked about it. Love in my house was never bubbly or physical when we were young, but it was there all the time.

My dad traveled a lot for work, and although looking back I know he loved us all, I judged him for not being around. But I also respected him for giving us what he had to give. We were poor and I wanted to blame that on him. He was there for birthdays and special occasions, but his work kept him away, and that made me blame him for everything to an extent. Especially when I couldn't see his efforts and sacrifices, but I could see my mother's. She lived a typical Latin life, caring for her family and husband. I didn't realize that at the time he compromised too. But my mom struggled in front of us to make ends meet, and our situation was a sad reality that many Latin families encountered.

Their relationship deteriorated little by little, year after year. We were stuck in that building in the middle of a tremendously impoverished part of town. My dad was off doing other things most of the time, leaving my mother to raise six kids with very little. When I think about what we used to eat for dinner, it was always pork. My mother would generally fry it, and if we had bread, then we'd have a sandwich with pork—ham and some cheese. She'd buy seven pieces, but some nights, Limayri would get up late at night and make herself one piece. So when dinnertime came the next day, I remember many meals where there was no meat on my mother's plate. There was no money left to buy more. Eventually I stopped eating pork altogether because it just reminded me of those days, and we ate so much of it. Once in a very great while, we'd have an actual steak and that was a big treat.

The food was scarce, but because our neighborhood and our building were so poor, the water was even scarcer. We barely had any. No one could afford it on a regular basis. Once a week, or every few days when people cobbled together some money, the water truck would arrive. My mother worked so hard to keep the apartment clean and beautiful despite the shortage, but the building had become quite run-down. It got rough when we went many days without water, mostly because the bathroom would smell and the ants and cockroaches would get in. We couldn't flush the toilet too frequently, so the smell lingered. I had a hard time going to the bathroom, which made the smell seem worse as I'd sit in there for so long. My legs would fall asleep while I sat there, and I would actually do my homework to help pass the time. We could bathe, but usually with cold water, using a bucket of water for washing.

When the truck, or sometimes two trucks, would occasionally pull up (we knew that everyone in the building had collected extra money when there were two), we'd hear the engine coming up our little hill, and when it did, we all sprang into action. Everyone had a job, and we had to move fast. We'd hear the pipes getting filled. We'd open up all the faucets in the house, but because we were on the fifteenth floor, we'd get less water than everybody below. Once the water started flowing, I would wash the dishes while one of my sisters would dry. My brothers would fill buckets and put them everywhere so that we could save some for bathing and dishes later in the coming days. My mother would clean up the bathroom. We usually had ten minutes once the truck had filled the building's tanks to get it all done, using every drop we could get out of the taps.

My mom made our apartment nice despite our poverty. In Venezuela the streets outside might be riddled with litter, but inside we kept our homes impeccably clean. My mom would compensate for the outside conditions with tons of plants inside, and we had beautiful wooden furniture from Mexico. So even though there were little lines of ants that we could never get ahead of, she made a pretty space for us and kept it ultraclean.

One thing my dad did give us all, which was very important to him and to us, was an education. So while we lived in rough conditions, we went to a really good school, which became more of an issue socially than we ever told our parents because while we had no money, everyone else at the school had a lot of it. We had to take the RUTA 6 bus to get there. The bus was usually reserved for maids and really poor people like us. There was no greater evidence of a social divide than when it came to transportation.

I felt how poor we were even though we all wore uniforms. I pretended at first to be Mexican; it was self-preservation. "Pretended" is perhaps a notion I thought of later upon reflection, because in truth we had learned to speak Mexican Spanish. So we didn't even sound Venezuelan, my brothers and sisters and I. We sounded Mexican, and that worked well for us at this school. I used that, in part because I felt like such an outsider, but also because I knew I was different from everyone else at school and didn't want that divide to be about money. We made it about Mexico instead, though I learned later everyone had their struggles in life. Mexico sounded foreign enough to be almost sophisticated and special. So even in my home country where I was born, I was always out of place somehow, wanting to escape my reality. Being "Mexican" helped mask my feeling of not belonging. It was just too harsh to face the reality: that we were broke and on the bus. My brothers, though we never discussed it, played the secret role somewhat too, mostly because they were really good at soccer and the kids even referred to them as the "Mexicans" on the field. My brothers never corrected them.

It got so bad that, after coming out of school and walking to take the bus, which picked us up a few blocks away, I would hide behind one house's fence, ducking down so no one could see where I was waiting to go home. The other kids were picked up in cars and driven home. I had to walk past them to get to the bus, across the avenue. I'd watch car after car go by, and I'd occasionally even let a bus go by so that no one from my class would see me getting on it. I would hide and wait, and the second a bus came and no one else was driving by, I would run very fast and get on that bus. I had an aunt who lived very close to the school. If I bumped into someone while I was heading to the bus, I would say I was going to my aunt's house to explain why I was on foot.

Most days, as I crouched down behind that fence, I didn't dare even dream that I'd get out or think that I'd have the chance to do anything but live the way I was living. That was the life I knew. Still, I never felt anchored there or anywhere. I almost always had a feeling I didn't belong, no matter where I was. For some reason I was an outsider at the core and that feeling may have had something to do with how my life eventually turned out. I didn't know it so much at the time because I lived with that feeling, that outsider feeling, daily. I didn't know until much later exactly why, but I knew I felt it, like it was always a struggle.

Chapter Three

Growing up, I escaped through dance and was a member of a company in some capacity from the time I was five years old. It was quiet and safe, a space where it was okay to just be, move, and not have to work to fit in. I felt at home with the dance company and onstage. It might have been the one place I felt I belonged and where having no money really didn't matter. I just danced to dance—never seeking approval even onstage, always hoping to touch the audience or even just one person through artistic expression. The movement, the music, the expression—I loved losing myself in all of it. It was a wonderful, happy place for me. I don't remember ever not dancing. I went almost every day from three o'clock to six o'clock, which made me different from the rest of the kids at school because I didn't participate in a lot of the other activities they did, and I had to study after dance.

In addition to the artistry, I learned discipline and dedication, which carried me through my life and career. I won't say I fully agreed with the methodology at the time; when I was fourteen years old, I had one strict director, Miss Soraya, who made us all step on a scale daily when a trip was approaching. I didn't know what it was at the time, but looking back, it is clear that some of the girls I danced with were bulimic or anorexic. I never fell that deeply into the dieting. It was an important dance company, so we abided by the director's strictness and didn't eat what other young teen girls were eating—nothing fried, no *pastelitos* with *carne* or *queso*. There were seven or eight of us, and we all had different lead roles in different numbers, but if one person gained a few pounds, we knew someone in the wings was rehearsing our part, ready to replace us. The director would simply pull you if she wanted to, and she often did. But I stuck it out. It was an enormous opportunity for most of us. We traveled all over Latin America to perform, seeing places we'd never otherwise have had the opportunity to visit. We loved travel for two reasons: we got to see new cities, and we weren't weighed while we were on the road. That meant we were allowed to eat whatever we wanted. I remember one trip in particular to Mexico City, standing in a park after a show with my sister and my future sister-in-law Laura, and we ate seventeen tacos. *Seventeen.* Because we knew the director wasn't going to check our weight until we returned home and were in rehearsals.

At one point, a trip to Aberdeen, Scotland, was being discussed at rehearsal and we were all really excited about it. Only some of us would get to go, however, and that had everyone on high alert. I was excited about the trip and fairly certain I would be chosen. I worked hard. Visiting Europe seemed liked something so far out of reach for most of us that we couldn't even imagine it. Dance, and the trips, made us forget our poverty, and getting to see Europe would have made any one of us feel something incredible. Around the same time the prospect of Scotland was buzzing; perhaps because our reputation as a troupe was growing and we were getting new opportunities, our director was reaching new levels of ugliness—almost becoming abusive. Some girls had come and gone as a result of the pressure she placed on us to starve ourselves, including my sister, who found it far too strict and stressful, even though she was the skinniest one among us and had the least to worry about in terms of getting fat.

One afternoon, my friend Teresa's mother picked us up after rehearsal. The director had been particularly evil during the weigh-in, and we were explaining this to Teresa's mom as she pulled out of the parking lot.

"She told me I was fat," Teresa said. "She told us we had to stop gaining weight to get Scotland."

"You are young girls," her mother said, watching the road. "That's a lot of pressure. You're still developing." She seemed concerned. "Patricia, is your mother worried? Should we get a few of us together to talk about it?"

About a week later, we convinced six or so girls and some of their mothers to meet in Teresa's living room. It was bright because of the many windows, but I remember thinking that it was very brown inside.

The wooden pieces were dark brown, the couch was brown, and the curtains were brown. But there was this big glass window overlooking a terrace, and it created brightness despite the decor. I felt nervous because we were meeting to come up with a plan to stand up to our director. Many people were sitting, but I stood in front of the big window, pacing back and forth a little as we collected our thoughts.

"We can't be starving ourselves, and we can't be rehearsing so many hours anymore," one of the girls said. "Everybody is getting injured."

I thought for a moment. I decided I needed to be the one to speak up on behalf of us all. I looked down at the carpet to think about what I should say. The carpet was plush and thick. I had bare feet, beaten up from dancing. I looked down at them, thinking that the carpet must be thick for my feet to sink so deeply into it that they half disappeared. After pausing I said, "I'll do it. But just so you know, it's not that I mind confronting her. I don't. But what if she kicks me out?"

"We'll all quit," someone else said. "If she does that, we'll all quit. She'll have no group left." These were strong, smart girls. They wanted to dance, but they wanted to be healthy too.

Side conversations erupted, and everyone was nodding and discussing things at the same time. I interrupted, "Guys, guys. Okay. If you'll all walk out with me if it goes bad, I'll do it tomorrow. I'll speak up."

We came up with some things I should say to make our point. Everyone thanked me as they were leaving. I was going to change things for the better, fix a problem. I felt empowered by the support, terrified at what had to be done, and excited to make everything better for everyone. Still, I didn't sleep that night, knowing that what I had to do would be difficult. But I knew it was important. I'd been given a mandate, and I wouldn't let people down.

We arrived at the studio after school the next day as planned. After we rehearsed, some of the girls were giving me looks and nodding, telling me it was time. I looked at our dance director while I gathered my thoughts. She was thin. Not too tall. Bony. She was curt and aggressive in almost everything she said. With everyone cooling down, I swallowed hard and said, "Miss, can we talk?"

I paused. Then I spit it out. It was like one long sentence, but it was hundreds of words spoken faster than I'd ever have spoken them normally. It was adrenaline. I was so afraid that I mixed up my words; they all just spilled out of my mouth in some random order. I don't even remember each thought. I just blurted out one big prepared speech.

When I stopped, the room was silent. Some girls were looking at their feet, while others showed solidarity by standing cross-armed. I wasn't sure if some had lost their nerve, but I feared a few of them had. I stared straight at the director, trying not to show fear. I told her that we were worried, that we were growing and the weight was just from developing, not fat, that we couldn't help it, but that we loved dancing and working hard. I kept looking around, waiting for some backup from the others, but nothing. No one said a word. After what felt like an hour but was only a few seconds, the director said, "Leave." She didn't even look me in the eye, just flung her hand in disgust and spun around to go.

"Why?" I asked, even though I knew the answer.

She stopped at the doorway before leaving the studio. "Leave. If you don't like it, leave the group. Consider this your last rehearsal."

One brave supporter said, "If she's out, I quit." And she collected her things. The director said, "Great, anybody else?" Then she walked out.

Stunned, no one else said anything. Not Teresa, not the others who had promised. No one. I didn't say another word. I grabbed my bag and ran out. As I descended stair by stair, my eyes filled with water, and then the tears burst out almost all at once. I thought about what had led up to this and realized that Teresa's mother had wanted me out all along. This had been a setup so that Teresa—who had always had some weird obsession with me and all I had achieved, I realized only in retrospect—could go to Europe. I was so foolish to have believed everyone. As I passed the director's truck, I decided to do something bad. I looked around and, without even thinking, kneeled down and let the air out of the tires. Then I hurried to the corner to wait for my mother to pick me up where she usually did. I'd been badly betrayed, and I was angry with myself. At least I'd get to eat what I wanted now, but still, I knew nothing else that gave me as much joy as dancing. It was everything, and now it was gone. As I waited for my mother, two of the girls, Josefina and Sabrina, caught up with me. I could barely look at them. I wiped away the tears as I listened.

Josefina spoke for them both. "Listen, Patricia, we will never get to go to Europe in our lifetimes. Would you hate us terribly if we just did the trip and then quit? This will be our only chance for a trip like that. You know how we live. We promise, once it's done, we're out."

I actually did understand, and I appreciated how concerned they appeared and how conflicted they must have felt. They looked truly sad and broken by what had happened.

"Yeah," I said. "I'd be happy if you went. You should do it. It's the right thing. You've earned that trip. I want you both to go."

We all hugged, and my mom pulled up to get me. I told her what had happened, and I think she was more devastated than I was—and I was crushed.

"I shouldn't have let you be the one to speak up," my mom said. "I'm so sorry, Mija."

I didn't realize it at the time, but this was an important moment for me. My actions that day in dance—stepping up, speaking up for others, dedicating myself to a cause, and leading by example—were standards I had set for myself. That was a pivotal moment for me. Even though it burned me at the time, I still felt good about what I had said. It still felt good to take action and speak out against an injustice. It felt good to lead.

Josefina, Sabrina, and one other girl did quit after Scotland. So Miss Soraya lost four dancers, including me. Not Teresa—she stayed on and became the lead in the company. It was a betrayal, sure, but I should have seen it coming. I had always had a bad feeling about Teresa, but I didn't listen to my instinct. That was one lesson learned. And as I discovered many times over later in life, good things often came of terrible situations. I would frequently get knocked down, but I would always get back up stronger.

Months later, a few of us formed our own contemporary dance company. It was amazing, and we had fun being fat, and good, and not having the pressure of the overbearing director. And from that energy we became extremely talented. The positivity and the new vibe with an amazing new teacher named Paola transformed us all. It was one of the first times I understood art as collaboration and not as a form of discipline. When I was young, it always seemed like everything was dire, but this new dance company was one of the first times I realized that life could work out for me, that I was strong, and that perseverance paid off. I studied engineering and I danced. I never did make it back to Europe to dance, but that was okay. The contemporary dance group had changed me for the better, and I couldn't have been happier with the turn of events.

Chapter Four

"*Hola*, Patricia." I knew instantly it was *him* before he said his name. His voice was strong and beautiful. I felt chills when I heard it. "It's Ernesto. How are you?"

"Good," I lied. I was a bundle of nerves. "I've been waiting for you to call me."

"I know. I'm sorry. We left very late, and then we came here, to Caracas. We're leaving for Ecuador tonight," he said.

"No way," I said. My heart sank. "I want to see you again."

"I want to see you too. But I'm here and you're there."

There was a pause on the line.

"You can come meet me for a short time in Caracas at the airport. That's the only way."

My mind was racing. I was considering how I could make that work. I wondered if he was only joking. He wasn't.

"Why don't you? We're going down to the airport. We can meet there, even if just for a bit."

I started flipping through strategies in my head. I knew from traveling with the dance company that there were many flights from my town to Caracas, like every two hours. I figured if I could take the six o'clock, I could return on the ten o'clock flight and no one would even know. I needed money, though; that was the problem. The ticket would be expensive. I had none.

"Yes!" I said. I'd find the money. "I'll be there. I'll be on the flight at six.

Be waiting where I arrive, okay?"

He agreed, and I raced to make my plan a reality. Considering we had no cell phones at that time, and I was just fifteen, the plan was truly insane. Foolish too, but I was too young to know or care. I was so drawn to this guy that I couldn't resist. I hung up before I changed my mind and ran into the room I shared with Limayri and my younger sister, Caty.

Caty knew I was up to something as soon as I flew into the room. There was a small terrace at the back of our room where we would study. She looked up from the book she was reading for her homework. I stood before her, inadvertently putting my hands in a loose prayer position.

"I have never asked you for this before, but you've got to help me." I explained what I was going to do. "I have to get on that plane."

"Of course, Patricia," she said. No hesitation. Caty was a saver. So every penny she earned, she put away in a box under her bed. She pulled the box out and gave it to me without even a thought. I promised to pay her back, though I'm not sure I ever did. When I came out into the living room, my mother was in the kitchen getting dinner ready.

I hesitated, then came up with a lie. "Mamá, I'm feeling better. I want to go to Tamara's house to study, catch up on what I missed today." I'd always been so straightforward with her that she didn't even hesitate before saying, "Okay." She was stirring something on the stove and didn't even look up. It pained me that she had such blind trust in me, and that if she knew I was lying, she'd think so poorly of me.

I ran back into the room and got ready, making myself feel as pretty as I could. I even pulled a pair of heels, which I rarely wore, out of the closet and put them in a bag so my mother wouldn't get suspicious. I snuck into her room to call a cab, whispering as I ordered. I moved slowly out the door, but once in the hallway I ran, got in the elevator, and headed to the airport.

Looking back, it's amazing I was even allowed to board. I was a minor, after all. But in heels and considering how tall I was already, I must have looked much older. And talk about an excruciating fifty minutes in the air. All I could think was: *What if he isn't there when I get there? What would I do, having flown all that way?* I could hardly breathe with anticipation. As I sat on the crowded plane, I would calm myself down, take a breath, and say in my head, *He'll be there. He'll be there.* He had to be there. I'd felt his honesty and sincerity when we spoke. I had to trust my gut, which said he'd be there. I probably should have been scared, but I wasn't. My judgment was overruled by the fact that I needed to see this man. When the plane landed, I was jumping out of my skin.

I came out of the gate, walking, trying not to look overly eager but moving quickly—toward the baggage claim, which was the only way to go. I expected to see him waiting as soon as I stepped off the plane, so I was somewhat disappointed when he wasn't. I looked at all the people walking or waiting, hoping to spot him. I didn't see him as my eyes frantically scanned the crowd. He should have been standing closer to where I would arrive. No one was looking for me in Caracas. That was clear. I felt deflated and dumb for thinking he would be there. I slowed my pace a bit but kept going a little farther anyway, feeling like I'd just wasted my time and a lot of money. I was angry at myself, sad about not seeing him. Why would this guy take the time to meet with me anyway?

Just as I was about to cry at my foolishness, I turned a corner and saw him there waiting, right by where the suitcases were dropping out onto the belt—the baggage claim for the people taking my flight. It was the most beautiful thing I had ever seen. His faded jeans clung tightly to his body. His cowboy boots were perfectly scuffed to match his scruffy hair. His longish black leather jacket had some scruff to it too. It wasn't grungy; it was edgy. Rock and roll.

I could not believe he was there.

I took in the sight of him as I breathed, absorbing every inch of him. He smiled when he saw me. I wasn't shaking. I was just thinking, *I am in love with this man.* I certainly didn't know much about love at all. I should have been thinking, *This guy is famous and probably has a hundred girls in every port.* But I wasn't. I figured if there were other girls after him, I was clearly at the top of his list. Why else would he take this time to be with me?

I walked up to him and just smiled brightly when I arrived. He wrapped his arms around me, and we stood there hugging for a minute. He didn't kiss me on the lips; he was very respectful, probably because of my age, and I think we both knew a kiss would have been disrespectful. He was a lot older than me. Like more than double my age.

We exchanged just a few words—how are you, how was your flight?— nothing deep. And after what felt like a second or two but was probably fifteen minutes, some people traveling with him came to get him. We hadn't even left the spot by the baggage claim, and he was leaving to catch his own plane already.

"We're going to Ecuador now," he said. "It is so crazy that this worked." He touched my shoulder softly, but only for a second.

"There's no way I could let you leave for Ecuador without seeing you first. Especially since I don't know if I'll ever see you again." It was all happening so quickly that I felt crushed, though I knew it would never be much more than this.

"I'll write to you," he said. "I promise."

"Promise?" I asked.

"Promise."

And after one more tight hug, the man I was so instantly in love with was gone. I absorbed what I had just experienced and done to see this guy and watched him catch up to his bandmates and head for the plane. He looked back once and waved through the crowd. I gasped when he did. I was so happy that I just stood there smiling for a couple of minutes, even after he was out of my sight. All I wanted to do was see him again.

With a little extra spring in my step, I made my way quickly to the departures counter to check in. I had two hours or so until the last flight left. I waited in line, and when I got to the front of the line, I almost died.

"I'm sorry," the woman behind the counter said. "The last flight out was canceled."

I just stared at the woman. I didn't know what to say. I knew I was in trouble.

"There's a six a.m. flight," she said.

The next day. This was bad. I nodded and said, "Yes, put me on that, please."

She handed me a ticket, and I slowly stepped away from the counter, bewildered and downright terrified. I knew I couldn't stay overnight at the airport because that would be very unsafe. I sat in the first seat I found to think as everyone coming and going for the last few flights of the evening hustled by me. Whom did I know in this city? No one. I'd gotten myself into a major mess.

I remembered that a year before I had been traveling with the dance troupe, and I sat next to a journalist on the plane—a big, fat, old guy named Victor. He was the only person I knew or could think of. He had said at the time, "If you ever come to Caracas, please give me a call." He gave me his card, which I'd stuffed into my wallet. At this point it was nine o'clock already, and I was starting to get really scared. I had pretty much zero money with me, just some change. I knew I had to go somewhere, and soon. I didn't want to call my mother, but I knew I'd have to come up with some sort of lie to explain why I wasn't going to make it home. This would be the first time, other than when I'd traveled with the dance company, that I hadn't slept at home with my family.

I had to shake off my fears. It was time to plan. I got up and walked to a phone booth outside the terminal where people got dropped off. Everyone was smoking out there, and it smelled like exhaust and cigarettes. I wasn't sure if it was the smell that made me sick or the lie I was about to tell. I had enough money to make two calls. I dialed home first.

"*Hola.*" It was Limayri, my older sister. I'd caught a break.

I unloaded. I told her I was at the airport and what I had done, and that I had to take the first flight in the morning.

"What are you going to do?" she asked.

"I'll figure out something, but tell Mamá I'm still at Tamara's and will just sleep here because we are still working."

I heard a clicking noise on the phone. "The money is running out. I need to go."

"Okay, but you never sleep over. She will wonder," she said.

Then I heard my mother. "Patricia? Is she on the phone?"

She came on the line. "Patricia, where are you?"

I was frantic. "Mamá, we're still working. I'll just stay, okay? I never do it, but it will be fine. "

The lies were coming so easily, and she believed them without question. I had given her no reason in the past not to. "Okay, Mija. You stay. Don't worry."

And with that, we hung up. I had never lied to *that* extent before. I felt worse than I'd ever felt. Dirty. Ashamed. But I had little time to dwell on my despair, so my survival instinct kicked in.

I dug through my wallet and found Victor's card. I used my last bit of change to call, hoping he would be there. I dropped it in the machine and dialed.

Ring.

Ring.

I was sweating.

If he wasn't there, I was in trouble. As the phone rang I thought of my mother and how terrible I felt about the conversation we'd just had. It hurt, physically hurt, to think of what I'd done and said.

"Hello," he said when he finally picked up.

"Hello," I said, reminding him how we'd met. "I have a little bit of an issue. I'm stuck at the airport. My flight was canceled, so I can't go home until the morning."

"Oh God, Patricia," he said. "You can't stay there. It's not safe. I'll come get you. I live very close to the airport."

"Thank you," I said relieved. He sounded genuinely worried.

"I have a Monte Carlo, blue and black. I will be there in fifteen minutes."

I didn't know I was about to make one of the worst decisions of my life.

I knew the second I hopped into Victor's car that he was drunk. I could smell it when I opened the door to get in. Fortunately, this guy didn't live in central Caracas, which was very far from the airport. He lived on the outskirts nearby in a newish neighborhood that was closer to the airport. It was oddly isolated, one building alone, protected by mountains. There was nothing else around. That's what I was thinking as we approached it shortly after pulling away from the airport curb. It was like a little collection of lights amid the darkness. I hadn't given it much thought when I made the call, but as we drove, it became pretty clear from this guy's enthusiasm that he thought something was going to happen between us. He was staring at me like he was looking at a roasted chicken he was about to devour, stopping short of licking his lips. It was creepy. He clearly lacked respect. He looked to be about fifty and must have known I was a young teen.

It wasn't until we got up to his apartment door, where there was some light, that I noticed how pasty white he was. He had thick black hair and looked fatter behind the wheel of the car, but standing up, he was clearly a big man with a big belly. He wobbled as he fumbled for his keys. I might have been on higher alert any other day, but thoughts of Ernesto were still swirling in my head. Love had blinded me to any danger, clearly.

He opened his front door on the seventh floor, but he let me go in first. Then he entered and double-locked the door behind him, using a key that he put in his pocket. He was chatty and stayed close to me when he spoke.

"Why are you here in Caracas?" he asked.

"I came to see a friend," I said. I didn't want to tell him too much because I felt like it wasn't his business. And I also had to protect my man because he was famous. Plus, I liked that our meeting had been a secret between Ernesto and me.

As I spoke, I took a quick glance around the place. The living room was decorated with lots of bright colors, overcrowded with furniture and porcelain everywhere. Despite it being like any other home I'd entered in Venezuela, I was suddenly feeling a little worried about my surroundings. He walked toward a doorway that led to his bedroom. I think he thought I was going to follow, but I took a step toward the kitchen in the other direction as if I was just looking around a bit. On the other side of the kitchen was another room.

I made up something quickly to further explain my trip and keep talking. "I had to bring him, my friend, some papers he had forgotten in Maracaibo. And then the plane got canceled, so I got stuck."

I could see into that little room behind the kitchen. A man and a woman were sitting on their small bed watching TV. I wasn't sure, but I assumed they were either the maids or renting the room from him. I was relieved. I wasn't alone. They seemed shy or embarrassed; they started speaking more quietly and didn't really acknowledge me. I walked into the kitchen to be nearer to them.

He cut past me and said something to them in a low voice that I couldn't hear and then shut the door. There was a clicking sound too, as if they had locked it. I sat on a chair in the kitchen. It felt like a safe place to stay—one where I could remain all night if necessary. He grabbed a bottle of whiskey and poured a glass, which he drank in one gulp and then poured another. He put a glass in front of me, but I said, "No thanks. I don't drink. I'm too young."

He pulled a chair close to me, seeming aggressive and really drunk, as if he'd held it all together driving but his drunkenness had just come back to him quickly. A few things made me feel okay about the situation: First, he was drunk, which meant I was sharper. Second, the couple in the back room would hear if I screamed. I also considered that, as a dancer, even though I was long and lean, I was strong and fast. He was old and fat and stumbling. I'd lifted guys while dancing, so I started to calculate how I could push back if this guy got in my face.

"I'll be right back," he said. He left the kitchen, and I began snooping around a bit, making myself aware of my surroundings, checking the door first to see if I could unlock it. I couldn't; I needed the key. Then I wandered into the dining room to see if there was a spare key in a dish on the cabinet. Nothing.

Suddenly, standing in the dining room was this fat man, wearing only his underwear. Though I was cornered, I didn't move, but I thought, *If I just play him, this man will pass out.* I'd seen a lot of drunk people, mostly family members at gatherings, by this point in my life, so I knew what came next. They always stumbled, and this would be no different.

"Where's the key to the front door?" I asked. "In case of emergency."

"It's in my bedroom."

Then he headed there. Relying on the knowledge that I could take him, I followed. I felt I needed the key in my possession. When I entered he was on the bed, and when I walked in, he held up the key, shook it, and dropped it into his underwear. It was so gross, but I giggled. I was happy to play along because I was going to win.

"Come over here," he said, coaxing me toward the bed.

When I didn't move toward him, he got up and grabbed me. Not so hard at first, but then he pulled me toward him, pressing himself up against me. I tried to pull away, but he was holding me tightly, groping me with one hand—my face, my neck, making his way down to my shoulders. I was freaking out inside but tried to remain calm.

"Just let me go to the bathroom, and then I'll be right back, okay?" I said.

"Take your time. I'll be here waiting."

When I was young, I used my charm to get things I couldn't afford. We had no money, so I learned quickly that my charm and apparently my looks (I wasn't at all aware that I was pretty) could help me. I used to love dulce de leche ice cream. I couldn't afford it, but I always got it by flirting just a little with a boy who could.

I hoped my charm would work on this man, or I would be in trouble. I wasn't looking for ice cream, just my safety. I gave a little wave and said, "Great."

I stepped out and waited outside the door, listening to his breathing. I tiptoed to the couple's room, knocking lightly.

"Can you help me?" I asked in a hushed voice.

Nothing.

"Please open the door. This guy is going to rape me."

The man opened the door a crack and said, "We can't help you." He was frightened and had clearly been warned against aiding any of this gross pig's conquests.

"Can I just have a key? To leave?"

He shut the door on me.

Plan B. I tiptoed back to the bedroom door to listen. Within minutes his breathing became even louder, harsher sounding. I had to make my move and be fast about it. I peeked my head through the bedroom door; sure enough, he had passed out from the booze. In what felt like one move, clutching my purse, I sprung in, stuck my hands into his underwear, and grabbed the key. I darted directly to the door and let myself out, tucking the key in my pocket as I ran. I moved like lightning down several flights of stairs.

There I was, in the middle of nowhere. All I had was a purse. I couldn't go out and walk anywhere because there was nothing outside. I peered outside the front door of the building, remembering we'd passed a guard coming in. I walked over to his booth and said, "I've got to get out of this place. I need to leave. I need to go to the airport. How do I get there?"

"Oh, you are so far away. You will have to take a bus that leaves here at six in the morning."

"Not until six?" I asked.

He nodded. The flights came every two hours. I could catch the eight o'clock.

"I want to leave now. Is there any way?"

"You're in the middle of nowhere." This was a new neighborhood and a new complex in the middle of the mountain. Just mountains and one building, like the start of a new suburb.

"What about a taxi?" I asked, even though I knew I didn't have the money to pay for a taxi, and at this hour the airport wasn't safe either.

"It's too early in the morning. It won't be safe even to drive there."

"Okay, thanks," I said and headed back into the building. I went up the stairs, but only a few flights. I balled myself up in a dark corner, waiting and watching. I would not sleep. I was worried the fat guy would wake up. If he did, I'd have to run. I knew my safest bet was to stay on this floor, down low and near the stairs. He'd never take the stairs.

At one point in the night, I heard screaming and knew it was him. "Where are my keys? Where is she? You let her out." It pierced the quiet air, making me shake. The apartment was very open and airy. His voice carried through the halls and floors.

It silenced eventually. I figured he'd passed out again. As I sat there, crunched up in a corner absorbing the quiet, I thought about my mom and how ashamed she'd be of me at that moment if she knew, and how sad she'd be that I'd done this. I hoped I'd get out okay so my mom would never find out I'd lied or put myself in a stupid situation to begin with. My eyes filled with tears. Here I was doing this reckless thing. If my brothers knew, they would have killed this guy.

As dawn was breaking, I heard another voice, this time a little kid—a toddler of three or so, I guessed. I heard a man talking to her. I figured since there was a kid, I would be safe. I darted down the flight of stairs to where the voice was coming from and approached this young man, holding hands with his daughter, struggling with a big bag and backpack. This was my ticket out of there.

"I need help," I said. "It's a very long story, but I need to get away from this building and get to the airport."

"I can't take you all the way to the airport, but I'll get you to the bus. Is that okay?" He seemed very concerned as he looked around to see if I was alone.

I nodded. I didn't want to tell him much, but I knew I was okay with him because he had a child. He offered me money for the bus. Just before boarding that bus, I tossed the stolen key onto the side of the road. Later that morning I finally got on the plane home. As I flew, I knew I could never tell anyone what had happened. This was the moment in my life when I lost the childlike trust I had been born with. It was a turning point, the groundwork for many mistakes and bad decisions to come. It was the start of hiding truths, feeling shame, and losing trust in people. A few more lies and by evening it was as if none of it had even happened. It had, though. And as I tried to fall asleep that night, I wondered if it all had been worth it. I didn't realize, probably because of my age or because I hadn't lied much up until that point, the true cost of a lie.

Though we secretly remained in touch for a month or so through phone calls and letters, and despite my certainty I was in love with him, Ernesto wrote to me one day to tell me he felt he was too old for me. He also had a girlfriend and was heading back to Spain to live. He said he had been moved by me, that he treasured our time together, but that it just didn't feel right. It was the girlfriend who made it easy to end it with him in my mind, end whatever we had and move on. When I received that letter, it felt like there was no way back. I was very sad. I couldn't cross that line, would never cross it. I would never be the woman on the side, the cheater. Never. I was desperate to see him, but not like that.

The turn my life had taken with him was over. I was devastated. I didn't respond. I just tossed the letter and, like any teenager would do, moved on. Never in my wildest dreams did I think I'd see Ernesto again in my lifetime.

Chapter Five

I had a recurring dream growing up that there was this tiny, narrow opening in one wall of my bedroom. I could barely squeeze myself through it sideways, even though I was thin. But once I slid through, I was able to edge my way down a dark tunnel that was only a few feet long and as narrow as the entry I had used to access it. At the end of the tunnel, right there behind the wall of my bedroom, was a giant pot overflowing with coins—shiny gold coins almost like what you'd see in a cartoon. Sometimes when I'd wake up from the dream, I'd think about whether or not there really could have been a pot sitting back there where I'd dreamt about it. I'd scan the wall to see if there was an opening that led to the tunnel. Or maybe I'd just hoped it could have been real—not even for myself, but for my mother. Deep inside, for as long as I could remember, I wanted to do everything I could to help her. She never complained or talked about how hard things were, never. But I knew she was stressed when she was quiet and at home, and that stress came from not having any money.

I remember one night while I was getting ready for bed, I accidently saw my mom getting ready too. I caught her in her panties changing. They had so many holes in them, I couldn't believe it. This remarkable woman didn't even buy herself new underpants because she bought them for us instead. Realizing I had no holes in my panties made me feel guilty to the core. She never spent a single penny on herself, not a penny. Deep inside, we all just wanted to do well so my mom would not have to endure this struggle anymore. We never talked about it with her or with each other, but I think we all felt the same way: it pained us all. I remember feeling the stress emanating from her on days when we couldn't attend classes because she didn't have the money to pay the school that week. We had to stay home while she figured it out. I dreamed I'd find that pot of gold one day. I desperately wanted to find it, whatever it took, so my mom wouldn't have to be spread so thin or work so hard.

We didn't have money for much else other than the necessities, but I remember saving for a very long time what little I had collected of my allowance and birthday gifts from uncles and relatives because I wanted to get a perm. I'd asked my mother if she minded my getting one and she didn't. She never wanted to deprive us of the occasional splurge. I'd seen pictures in some magazines and thought my thick black hair would look nice with some curl to it, even waves. I wasn't the kind of girl who usually cared about style and fashion and fluff, but for some reason I was stuck on getting a perm. So I made an appointment with a stylist named Jorge at a salon on this famous avenue in my town called Cinco de Julio. It wasn't a fancy place, but simple and unintimidating.

"Hi, I'm Patricia," I said as I sat in Jorge's chair. He put a black cape around me.

"Nice to meet you. Jorge," he said. His voice was high and his movements exaggerated. "What are we doing here today?" I'd never met anyone like him. He wore bright colors for a man and was more put together, less rugged, than most I'd met.

"I'd like a perm. Just enough to give me some waves."

"It will look horrible on you," he said bluntly.

"No. You think?"

"I know," he said.

"Let's just try. I've saved for it."

I was young at the time, probably fifteen. But Jorge treated me like an adult. I remember that. He made me laugh and was different from anyone I knew. He seemed so sophisticated.

I remember two things about the perm that day: the smell of the chemicals—which I kept thinking I should hate, but I really loved—and how horrible it looked when Jorge was finished. I wasn't pretty; I thought I looked ugly. I had dark skin and dark hair and was starting to lose my lankiness and grow curves. The perm didn't help matters.

Jorge didn't say, "I told you so." He just pursed his lips, raised his eyebrows, and said, "There's your perm."

I went back to Jorge many times after that despite the perm disaster because we grew to be friends and he cut my hair for free. It took a year or two to undo the perm's damage, and by then we'd become friendly—as friendly as a teenage girl and her hairstylist could be, anyway.

One afternoon, long after the perm had worked its way out, I was telling Jorge about a dance we'd been working on at my new dance company that had really moved me.

"It's so amazing, Jorge," I said as he cut my hair. "The orchestra for this is huge, and we're going to be performing in Teatro Teresa Carreño, the enormous concert hall in Caracas. There's one piece where we say, '*Mata, mata, mata* [kill, kill, kill].' We're killing our culture. We're killing nature. We're killing the indigenous people.'"

It had struck a chord with me, the dance. I was indigenous. I had grown interested in my Wayuu heritage as well. I'd been to the village many times to visit my aunts and cousins. Being there made us look rich by comparison; it was so poor there. We grew up with lots of strong women in this matriarchal society. The women were the bosses. That was the order there.

My aunt operated a line of buses, the only ones that went into the village. She ran it according to Wayuu law—an eye for an eye and a tooth for a tooth. When you hurt a Wayuu person, you had to pay. I saw my aunt deal with drunk drivers, for example. Once, a guy driving a car hit the bus and died. Even though he was drunk, my aunt's family had to pay or someone would have hurt her or someone in our family as payback. That's how it was. I remember another guy stumbling in front of a bus and dying, and my aunt had to pay then too. That was the nature of the law.

That region and that way of life, it all had a profound impact on me. I looked like everyone there—odd and dark, with my indigenous-looking eyes. These were my roots. I felt special being part of them, and I knew the nomadic, poor nature of the Wayuu coursed through me. Even though it was a lonely, hot, poverty-stricken place, it made me proud: I came from that. I was protected. I had a mission. It made me feel my existence wasn't a coincidence; the magic of the spirit of the indigenous people was a part of me, and it gave me the desire to move ahead in life. It was all about family and being part of a larger community. I grew up with this image of an old, spiritual man—not a real man, just one who protected and guided me, propelling me forward even through the most difficult times in life.

"We're raising awareness for our people through dance. It's so amazing," I said.

"You know how you could really raise awareness, Patricia?" Jorge slid a comb through a long, thin strand of hair and clipped the end before he finished his thought. He let the wet hair drop and said, "Entering Miss Venezuela. You've grown into such a beautiful woman since I've known you."

I laughed. "I'm not that kind of girl."

"Just think about it," he said. "You could be famous."

"I don't want to be famous. And besides, everyone who is in that contest is white. I'm too dark and way too curvy. I'm not pretty enough."

I laughed off Jorge's suggestion and went home that day. At the time I was planning to be an engineer, but I was also studying accounting. I didn't have a burning desire to be an engineer. My brothers were engineers and, because I was very good at math, it seemed the logical thing for me to do too. My passion was dancing, which I loved because I could express myself, but I didn't imagine it could become a career. Even though I knew my reality, I spent a lot of time in my dreams too, thinking up characters, imagining myself as someone who spoke English. The United States was sort of a fantastical, imaginary place to me, so thinking of speaking English as one of the characters in my head made me feel elevated, in my dreams at least, above my situation. I studied English at the time, but not enough to speak it. I couldn't really know what it would have felt like to have a conversation; I only imagined it. I often thought, *If I could speak English, I'd belong somewhere else, somewhere not oppressed, not less than. Somewhere happier.*

Every time I went in to see Jorge, he'd press me to enter the beauty contest. "Patricia," he'd say while he cut, "trust me. You should do this. I'll take you to Caracas. You're wasting time. I've done this for other girls."

This one particular visit, he got strategic about making a case for me to enter. A beauty contest seemed completely not my thing. I was boyish. I identified with being a guy in terms of wanting to win and lead, and I always felt guys had more privileges in life, especially Latin life. I tried to channel that somehow. Being a beauty queen and all dolled up with fancy hairstyles and makeup seemed out of whack. Dance wasn't girly to me. It was athletic. People admired dancers as artists.

"Patricia," he said, "I've heard you say so often that you want to help your family, that your mother works so hard and sometimes there is not enough food for the family. If we get you to Caracas for the contest, you could make money for her. A lot of money."

Miss Venezuela was always a big deal in my country: the Super Bowl of the nation. It was such an important part of the culture—giving opportunities to those who would otherwise have none. No matter what you thought of the notion of a beauty contest, it didn't matter; it created opportunity. The country would stop everything to watch this pageant. Being crowned a winner or even a finalist was a huge honor. So aside from thinking I wasn't made for it, I couldn't imagine I'd have a shot at it given how competitive it was. But as I sat there, I started to think: *What if Jorge is right? What if money follows?* Forget fame, forget all that. What if I made enough money eventually for my mother to put food on the table and get water for my building? I had no idea how the contest would unfold for me, but he'd finally said the right words to convince me to at least consider it.

"Let me give it some thought over the next couple of months," I said.

Then Jorge stopped cutting and walked around in front of my chair. He looked me straight in the eye. "You're wasting time. You have all these hopes and dreams of helping your mother with money. This is how you can help your mother with money. This is how you can free your mother from hardship. This is how you can help your family. This will put food on the table and water in the building. You might even be able to get your mother out of that building. I promise you, this is your opportunity," he pleaded with me, putting his hands on my shoulders as he knelt. "You do this, and I promise you, you can do whatever you want to do after. You will write your own ticket to fame and fortune, and you'll provide something for your family that will change their lives forever."

He dropped it right there in my lap, just like that. It was smart of him. He knew which buttons to push, and I didn't dismiss him. I promised to think it over, and I did. I left that day and even talked it over with my mother, who made a valid point that burst the pageant bubble: we couldn't even afford to send me to Caracas to try to get in. She was right. We didn't have the money to try.

The next day I went back down to Jorge's salon to explain. I entered his shop and waved to him. He was cutting someone else's hair, but he stepped away to greet me.

"Are we doing it?" he asked. He was excited, all smiles.

"Jorge," I said, "going to Caracas takes money. I'll need clothes and hotels and all that. I have no money for this. I talked it over with my mother, and she made the same point. We just can't afford to try. But thank you so much for having the confidence in me."

"I know we *can* afford it. I'll pay to get you there, to Caracas. I'll at least get us into a meeting and let them consider you. If they accept you into the competition, I'll find you a sponsor," he said. "I promise we can make this work." He was passionate about it, but it seemed too good to be true.

"Really? Are you sure we can pull this off?"

"Positive."

"Okay," I said. "Let's do it." I knew that getting in meant potentially quitting the university and the dance company, which I loved and adored, and I knew my mom would struggle with that. But if it worked out, and if Jorge was right, I could make something of it for sure. I was a hard worker if nothing else. If this opportunity materialized, I would run with it.

We all talked about it at home that night and my mother said, "Okay, Mija. If you want to do it, try." I promised her I'd finish school eventually.

When my brothers heard us talking about it and learned I was going to enter the Miss Venezuela contest, they had mixed reactions. Carlos, the jokester of the family, didn't just laugh; he was floored. "You? Really?" he asked. He was pretty—like, boy pretty. Gorgeous even. I wasn't. If I was, none of us knew it but Jorge. All my brothers were stunning. Me, I was rather ordinary.

My brother Juan was a little kinder about it. He was the sweet one in the family. He said to me later that night, "We'll be there for you if this is what will make you happy. If this is what you want, do it."

So I did. I was going for it.

Jorge's enthusiasm for getting me ready to compete was impressive, and I was grateful. To an extent I had become his muse, but mostly he was excited to launch into the business of managing talent. I was his start. He might have felt I had a chance, and while it meant a lot to me that he saw something in me I didn't see in myself, my trust in him meant something to him as well. He'd done this work with other girls, or tried at least, but he seemed grateful for our partnership.

His first task was to put me on a diet. For weeks I ate chicken with tomatoes and drank tomato juice. That was my diet. I lost a lot of weight too. Tomatoes were pure potassium, and when you added protein—well, I became really skinny.

Then we were off to Caracas to meet the Miss Venezuela program coordinators to see if they felt I had what it took to be groomed. Jorge booked us a hotel room, which we shared; it was weird, but since he was gay, he was more like a girlfriend. He never came out and said, "I'm gay," but he was open in other ways about it. You could be gay in our world, but you couldn't *say* you were gay. So we never discussed it. A gay person would have been an outcast in Venezuela, especially at that time. I'd certainly never met a gay woman.

Jorge styled my hair with a lot of volume for this important meeting. I just followed his lead. He told me he had done this with other girls, none of whom had made it into the contest, but he said the fact that he could get a girl into a meeting at all was a big deal. So I wore what he advised: massive high heels, big hair, a tight red dress, and lipstick that was brighter than I'd ever worn. I wasn't nervous because I didn't feel a burning passion to do what we were doing, but I was curious and giving it my all.

Jorge took me to an office building—the house of Miss Venezuela, or La Quinta as it was called—in Caracas to present me. We waited in the lobby until someone called us into an office. I carefully maneuvered in the high heels on my way in and sat as daintily as I could on a couch. Behind the desk in front of us was a guy, older but as impeccable and colorful as Jorge. He was the creator and the brains behind a legendary Miss Venezuela. His name was Osmel Sousa. Everyone knew who he was. He just stared at me as I sat there, his light-colored eyes assessing me. We all sat in silence while he looked. Eventually he stood up from behind his desk, never taking his eyes off me.

"Stand up," he said.

I did. He made a motion for me to spin around with his hand. He was serious, all business. I did.

Without addressing me, he said to Jorge, "Yeah, she's pretty. I like her." Then he went back and sat behind his big desk, took off his glasses, and continued, "Where is she from? Can she move to Caracas to be trained?"

My heart sank. I knew that meant money. But I didn't say anything; I let Jorge speak.

"Yes," he said. "We can figure that out. We'll get her here."

"Okay, good. We might need to do some retouching. Like redo those eyes. She'll need breast implants too. Her ears as well—we might need to do her ears. We'll figure all that out when you get here. Be back in three weeks. That will give us seven months to train for Miss Venezuela."

That was it. We left the meeting, and Jorge was so happy. I was happy, but I certainly wasn't getting all that surgery. Pondering the meeting as we headed back to the hotel, I thought about my eyes. I understood the breast implants. That didn't change me. I wasn't touching my ears. And I knew his suggestion to do my eyes was an effort to make me look like everyone else who competed in Miss Venezuela, but my eyes made me who I was—part of being Wayuu, and common, and indigenous. My eyes made me one of my people. Jorge and I talked about it as we drove, and I agreed to proceed only if the only surgery was my breasts. I didn't want to stop being who I was. I didn't want to let go of my roots and be an outsider in my own body. As much as I'd stared out at the people on the lake on the boats, I didn't want to lose my grounding and become them. My eyes meant something to me. And as much as I stared past the poverty, dreaming of gold coins, I was common and one of those people, and I wanted to hold on to that. My look, as weird and nontraditional as it was, represented all that for me. I had no way of knowing at the time, but years later my eyes would make me a success.

So we were going for it. I was going to walk on the biggest stage in my country, and I was doing it for my family. For Jorge it was a different kind of victory. I was the girl he had discovered who was going to be in the 1989 Miss Venezuela pageant. This would put him on the map. This was huge for him too. For me it was a means to an end, but I was up for the challenge and proud to get my chance to make something of us. From there, over the months that followed, things all happened quickly. My mom was behind the endeavor but also nervous, I could tell. And Jorge found a sponsor, whom I quickly learned was just an older guy who had the hots for me and was willing to pay my expenses in Caracas. Ultimately everyone in my family, myself included, knew this was a big deal. My sisters, brothers—we all knew what this really meant for the family. It meant prestige, and it potentially meant wealth. Deep down, beneath the nerves, we all felt it. We were excited. It gave me some hope that one day that pot of gold would be for real, not just in my dreams.

Chapter Six

In addition to finding me a sponsor, Jorge connected me with lots of people who could prepare me for the contest. One of them was a woman named Rossana, who had been named Miss Elegance in the contest the year before. One afternoon, while in my hometown for the weekend, Jorge and I went to a pizzeria owned by Rossana's father. Once I walked in, I remembered that my mother had taken me to the same restaurant years before. I recognized all the lightposts inside that made it look somewhat like a street in Italy.

Jorge and I were sitting at a table with a red and white checkered tablecloth, and this extraordinarily tall woman approached us. She was so tall and striking that I gasped when I saw her. She had the look—the look of a model. The look of a *Miss*. It was Rossana.

"Hello," she said.

I couldn't speak; I just smiled. Jorge introduced us, and I felt blown away by her beauty and dark hair. She was clearly Italian—her skin olive and glowing and perfect.

"I'm so short compared to you," I said, startling myself with the foolishness of the comment.

She laughed and said, "That's okay. We'll help you make up for it with everything else I teach you."

I was so excited that she was going to help me—thrilled actually, more so than I should have been or expected to be. She walked over and said something to the waiter and then came and took a seat. Her warmth radiated. My hand was resting on the table, and she took it and gave it a gentle squeeze. It was more than a squeeze: she held it for a moment before taking a sip of her water. Even the way she did that moved me.

We ate a little and talked, and I hung on her every word. Just speaking to her made me nervous. It was weird because I desperately wanted her to like me as much as I liked her. I knew from our conversation that night that she did. She was enthusiastic about me, I could tell, but I also gave her an opportunity to be back in the pageant environment. I knew I'd never love it like she loved it, but I was happy our connection had reopened a door for her.

The three of us met at my apartment before we were to head off to Caracas. After that first meeting I wanted her to be included in all that we did. More than Jorge, I wanted Rossana there. My excitement about her was greater than it was about the contest itself, and it made prepping for the contest bearable. We worked late that night. Jorge left while Rossana was on the couch yawning.

"Why don't you stay tonight, Rossana? I have a trundle bed in my room. We can pull it out," I said. "We have to get working again in the morning. Jorge will be back."

She thought about it for a moment and said, "Sure." We were giggly teens, and we were having fun. She called her dad and told him. I loaned her some clothes to sleep in and we set up her bed. She was going to sleep on the lower part of the bed and I above, but before we went to sleep, I wanted to lie down on the lower part of the bed with her. So we were face to face, talking very close on one tiny mattress. I don't even remember what we were saying; I just remember liking being close to her.

The door swung open. It was my mother, and she looked shocked.

"Oh, so sorry. I just wanted to give you some towels." She abruptly closed the door and left. Before she did, I jumped up onto my part of the mattress. Not that I felt I had been doing anything wrong, but I knew instinctively my mother had been put off by something.

The next morning, before Rossana got up, I was in the kitchen with my mother.

"Mija," she said, "what were you doing last night?"

"What do you mean, Mamá?"

"You were in the same bed as Rossana."

I was perplexed. I didn't really understand the problem, but I got the feeling my mother did. So I lied. "I just fell, Mamá. We were playing around."

She left it at that. But my head was swirling. Why was my mother so concerned? Why were my feelings so strong for Rossana? I had no idea what it all meant, but that moment definitely got me thinking that it meant something, because she had made a point of asking about it. I just didn't know what exactly.

Eventually we left for Caracas to start our adventure. We stayed in an apartment hotel, the Anauco Hilton, on our first night there. We booked one apartment with two rooms—one for Jorge and one for me. Rossana came with us, and I felt excited as we kicked off the arrival of my future and my quest to take on Miss Venezuela. We threw a little party in our room for our friends. It was a quick and simple celebration but perfect for what we were about to embark upon. Later, Jorge went to his room and everyone left. Rossana stayed in my room with me.

"That was fun," she said as she put some plastic glasses and other things into the tiny garbage can.

"It was!" I said. "I'm finally feeling excited about it."

"You should, you should. It will be great."

We both changed for bed and crawled in together. As odd as it seemed, as we lied there chatting I felt overly happy to be with her. I was confused, and I wasn't sure what she felt or if she felt the way I did. Never had one person stirred up so much inside me, but it was something I didn't understand. My feelings for Ernesto had been different, not physical or uncontrollable like this. Plus, the way my mother had reacted made me think it wasn't right. I felt mixed up. The look on her face in the apartment made me more conscious of what was going on than I had been, and more aware that something wasn't normal about how I was feeling.

That night Rossana and I held hands while we slept, or while we fell asleep at least. I woke up the next morning, and it was the first time I questioned whether it was okay to feel so strongly about Rossana. I was conflicted—ashamed for thinking about it at all and lonely because I was unable to say anything about it to anyone. She went back to Maracaibo the next day, and I kept on with Miss Venezuela. All I wanted was for her to come back, but she couldn't. I needed to let Jorge take the next step, which was to get me a sponsor. And that meant something altogether different for me.

Chapter Seven

I quickly learned that getting into the Miss Venezuela contest meant I would have to start prostituting myself in order to find a sponsor. Not everyone needed to go such lengths, but that was my reality. I knew I had an effect on guys and I used it, especially for this. With the help of Jorge, who was correct in saying that it wouldn't take long to find someone to pay for my stay and prep in Caracas, we found someone.

I can't remember exactly how I met him because Jorge had set up so many meetings, but David was a kind man, about fifteen or twenty years older than me. He fell for me immediately. He agreed to pay for me to stay and work toward the pageant. My initial reaction toward him was negative. He had a big face and a huge moustache. But I laid on the charm and he fell for it. He found me an apartment in Caracas and paid for breast implants.

I would see David weekly, in between the grueling training days when I'd learn to walk and how to carry myself, which came easily to me because of my dance background. As the weeks rolled by, I began to see that David genuinely seemed to care about me. He was tender in a way I'd never experienced, and he didn't pressure me immediately like I had assumed he would. I also never saw the money. Jorge handled it all. Still, I did my part. I kissed David as needed, accepting that I had to. That was the unspoken part of the deal.

A few months into the arrangement, he invited me away for the weekend to Margarita Island. I said yes, but I was uncomfortable and sickened when I realized, *I'm going to have to have sex with him.* The macho Latino society I'd grown up in made this seem like perfectly acceptable behavior—preying on young women, coercing them into having sex. As I was packing bikinis and lingerie, I remember thinking, *Fine, I'll have sex with you for your money. I can be just as ruthless. I won't get attached. This is a business transaction.* That was my thought process going into the weekend. It made me feel strong and empowered to think like this. It helped me rationalize what was happening and convinced me that what I was doing was just business. It was almost as if I'd created this resolve right then and there that no one was ever going to have control over me, that I was actually the person in charge, even though others might have had the money. That I was the one with the power. That I was never going to depend on anyone for anything.

David had this beautiful weekend arranged, and despite my stance on the whole situation, I couldn't help but feel and embrace the loveliness of his effort. He picked me up at my apartment and we drove to the airport. In the back of my mind, I thought as we traveled to our destination that my family would be ashamed of what I was doing to make this happen. I wondered if my mother knew what it meant to have a sponsor—or, rather, what I thought it meant to have one. After a short flight David and I arrived in paradise. I took in the palm trees swaying in the breeze and the scent of the sea, salty air, and sand. We checked into a beautiful hotel, and I felt at ease.

As much as I hated what I had to do to get what I needed, I realized that I was drawn to David, perhaps because he was older and somewhat fatherly. He made me feel protected and safe. That was something I had been craving. That weekend I saw in his eyes that he truly cared about me. After a day at the beach, he was especially loving and affectionate.

"Are you hungry? Are you too hot? Can I get you something to drink?" he asked graciously.

He gently stroked my arm. He pushed my hair out of my face. He was sweet and tender.

After dinner on the first night we would sleep together, I knew sex was inevitable. He hadn't said it, but he was determined, probably because of all the groundwork he'd laid.

I changed into a nightie and came out into our room. He was lying on the bed, but he was not naked or aggressive.

"Will you come lie with me?" he asked. "Would that be okay?"

"Sure, of course," I said. And I did. We kissed softly. He looked into my eyes, and for a long time that was all we did.

"Patricia, I love you, you know."

I was startled. He was revealing himself to be somewhat amazing and kind. "I love taking care of you," he said. It made me think that perhaps this man wasn't in it for the sex—that he'd really fallen for me. It was possible he really cared about me. We had gentle, loving sex that night, something I hadn't experienced with other boys. This was a man. A real man with love in his eyes. As I fell asleep that night, I realized I had to be careful. *You cannot fall for this guy, even if he really cares,* I thought, even though I was already falling just a little bit.

But David essentially became my boyfriend. I grew to feel for him. I didn't want to become completely attached, but I liked him a lot and he loved me. He was also incredibly kind and sincere with my mother when I did start bringing him around. My mom knew he had been brought in to help, but she didn't know the details of how it had started. He was sort of my boyfriend, but not one I ever told anyone else about. His kindness toward my mother made me feel for him even more. He was eventually around often, and I enjoyed his company. It made me feel protected. He remained a friend in later years, one I remembered with great fondness and appreciation.

Chapter Eight

What I remember most vividly about the night of the Miss Venezuela contest was how much my legs were sweating as I stood there in a heavy, long black dress with enormous shoulders and an explosive spray of wiry strings of silver sequins, waiting for results. I wasn't overly concerned about the results; we all knew who was going to win, and it wasn't going to be me. So after we'd worn these terrible red bathing suits cut way up high above our hip bones and satin-looking red mule shoes to match, and after we'd done all the typical pageant things, smiling until our faces hurt, we waited for the results all lined up. Some people were nervous, some were a mess because they had not been called, and some, like me, were just hopeful the night would pay off and something else would come of the hard work. When I finally heard my name called that night, all I could think was, *Okay, good. Now my life is about to change.*

I walked over to where I'd been told to stand, almost jumping the gun a bit as I realized from the buildup before they said my name that they were about to call me. I took my spot and looked offstage. Jorge was off in the wings behind a curtain, and he was weeping, just weeping with happiness. I didn't know how things were about to go, but standing there I knew I wouldn't be dancing or going back to study at the university. I could have and I would have, but I just had a feeling I was about to embark on something new. I also felt grateful that everyone who had made a sacrifice made it for a reason. The actual winner of the crown was sort of predetermined, and that was okay. I was a finalist, and that meant I got to be one of the *Miss Somethings* who went on to represent Venezuela at another pageant. Five were chosen, and when I heard my name, with the stage lights blazing on me and the crowd cheering, I knew I was one of them. I would represent my country at Miss Hawaiian Tropic. My giant hair and sweating legs gave me comfort. Comfort in knowing I had gotten it done and that the payoff would likely mean I could earn money for my mother.

The other payoff was that my family was beside themselves with excitement that night. It was a real honor and accomplishment to get on that stage, and I was aware even then that the pageant did great things for people like me who might not have otherwise had doors opened. Every girl in my country aspired to be a queen on that stage at some point in her life. Being chosen as a finalist brought such tremendous pride to the family, to my mother. This pageant comprised the biggest event in the nation. My mother, my sisters, and my brothers sat in a row in the audience, gleaming with excitement for me. And Jorge—he was so happy, it was palpable. He might have been the happiest of us all. He styled my hair that night, and with each touch-up, each updo, he was brimming with more excitement than I'd ever seen from anyone in my life. He was focused too, on it all. He wanted this. It was his dream. This night was almost more his than mine; that's how important it was to him. He'd tried to get other girls to where I'd just arrived, but none had succeeded. None had gotten him to the stage. None had actually competed, and none had had the potential to be a finalist. For me, the contest put me on an amazing path. Sadly for Jorge, his successes turned tragic much, much later in life. Still, in that moment, I was relieved that his sacrifices, my prostituting myself, had all paid off. All that fucking tomato juice too. I remember thinking that, whatever happened, I could eat whatever I wanted the next day.

I knew I didn't belong where I was going, but that was okay. I'd arrived on the stage, and that would get me somewhere that might feel more comfortable. I knew that. I'd made it for my family, for David, for Jorge, and for Rossana too. They'd done so much. It hadn't been for me, but that was okay. For me, I danced.

The good thing about not winning was that the contest wouldn't then own me. I was free to do other things. I owed them only one more contest, but that was it. I wasn't stuck. Had I been blonde and less curvy, sure, that might have been my fate. My looks were not typical enough to lock me into the pageant world, but they were certainly good enough to open a door.

Chapter Nine

Shortly after the contest, Rossana told me she'd be attending a post-pageant event where she expected to see a scout from Milan. He was choosing a girl to work for an agency in Italy. I figured I would go out eventually to similar castings, but I was surprised when, days after the pageant, Jorge called to tell me to get myself to the same meeting Rossana planned on attending. I was conflicted. She was a dear friend, and I knew from her enthusiasm that she wanted to be chosen. She had landed an appointment with Vittorio Zeviani, and she knew what she was doing. I was going in without any clue as to how to behave or any book to present, hoping to get into a room with him. I actually wasn't really hoping; I was going out of obligation. I would have preferred to wait for something else, something my friend didn't want so badly. I feared it would ruin our friendship. She'd been dating a guy named Luis, and that had already created some tension between us, as I didn't get along with him so well and didn't like how he pulled her attention away from me.

It's a little foggy to me how it all played out that day, how I got into the room with Vittorio Zeviani, mostly because as I sat there and eventually got called to see him, all I could think about was Rossana. But as soon as I did see him, he started asking me how I felt about Milan, where I was from, and how I would feel about moving overseas having just turned eighteen, I started thinking something else: *I'm never going back to dance.* I felt horrified thinking I was going to get Rossana's gig, but I had never seen a future for myself until that moment, never visualized anything but living at home. Caracas was overseas for me.

Days passed. I packed up my things in Caracas and headed home to my mother. Rossana was not patient as she waited for a call back. She called me all the time, telling me her dream to get to Milan to model—because, after all, she was Italian and that was where she wanted to land. It was everything to her. She knew I had gone, but not because I had told her; I never got a chance to speak to her about it. One afternoon, Jorge called and said Vittorio would like to come by and meet with my mother to talk about Milan. We agreed, but before the meeting we called the Miss Venezuela organization to verify that these people were legit and discovered they were. They were a significant agency, and they were coming to see us. I was getting my shot. My mother prepared some coffee, and when Jorge arrived with another man, we all sat down in the living room. Vittorio got straight down to business, looking directly at my mother as he spoke.

"We like your daughter. We would like for her to come to Milan and work as a model," he said. "We have picked her, and we'll pay for everything. She will just have to pay us back once she starts earning money, but there are a lot of girls who do it. That's how it works, and we can explain the financials to you."

My mother wasn't naive to the world. This was how girls were essentially kidnapped and sold into human trafficking. They met with agents who pretended to be legit, they were taken out of the country, their passports were taken, and then they had to work off the fees—not by modeling. It was terrifying and the sad, horrific reality of the world.

She looked scared but listened, not playing her hand in any way to suggest she would accept or let me go with them.

"Thank you for coming by," she said. "We'll talk about it tonight and get back to you in the morning. Is that fine?"

"Certainly," the agent said. And he politely left. Jorge walked him out.

She shut the door and didn't speak initially. Then I said, "Mamá, I've gotta do this. Think about it. If I can make even a little money, I can fill the building with water. Think about the money, Mamá. I've gotta get out there and make the money."

She was concerned. "I'll think about it, Mija," she said. "But this is not your burden. We will be fine."

But it was my burden, and it continued to be in my head. I needed to help my mother, my people, whoever needed it. If nothing else was clear to me in my life, that was. I wanted to provide what I could to help.

So I called Jorge right away to say my mom was worried. He returned immediately to impress upon her what a big deal this was, what an opportunity it would be. He also had some other news to deliver to us.

"Patricia was the only one who got picked," he said.

"Not Rossana?" I asked.

Jorge shook his head. "No. In all of this country, just you. No other girl got picked." I knew what that meant, and my mother did too: this opportunity was bigger than Miss Venezuela. Jorge left, and my mother promised she'd have an answer in the morning. We all ate dinner that night deep in thought. After dinner I knew I needed to call Rossana. I tried her number, but I couldn't get through. I left a message for her at the restaurant with her dad and at her apartment too.

Finally, at around 9:00 p.m. that night, the phone rang. I grabbed it on the first ring.

"Hello?" I said, hoping it was Rossana.

"Hello," a man's voice said. "It's Luis." It was Rossana's boyfriend.

"Oh, hi. Is Rossana okay?" I asked. "I've been trying to reach her."

"She's fine, yes. Out with some friends. Which is good because I wanted to ask you a question. Would you like to go out for dinner some night? With just me?" he asked.

The idiot asked me out. As if I'd hurt or betray Rossana like that. I was enraged. I knew Rossana loved this jerk. "How dare you call me? Your girlfriend is my best friend in the world." I slammed down the phone. I knew this wasn't good. I knew Rossana would be crushed that she wasn't going to Milan and that, worse, her boyfriend was hitting on me. She was going to hate me. I was frantic to speak with her, but despite my many calls, I couldn't track her down that night.

Later that evening, as I often did, I sat by the record player. I had two records that I played all the time, long after everyone had gone to sleep. I'd sit there in the living room, the apartment quiet, and listen to Supertramp over and over, even though I didn't quite understand the lyrics in English. My brother Carlos, who loved music, had given me the record. I smiled as I looked at my hand as I put the needle on the record. Carlos used to tease me about my hands. My sisters had beautiful hands, like my mom. I had my dad's hands. Carlos was always ahead of us all in a sense—the best looking, ultrasmart and talented. He never had to study, he was a supreme athlete, and he had that spirit that made people really like him. And he turned me on to Supertramp, which brought me some peace when I had thinking to do.

My mom came out in her nightgown. It was dark, with only the moon slightly illuminating the room. She said, "Let's go to sleep now, Patricia."

"No," I said. "I'm going to stay right here for a while."

"It's a big thing to go to Italy, you know. You just turned eighteen. You're very young. You don't speak Italian. You haven't finished your education."

"Mamá, this is a good opportunity. They chose me. Nobody else."

"How do we know that they're for real?" she asked. "What if they're pretending? And they take you and then you're gone?"

"Mamá, they are a very big agency." I knew we had no way to check, but the word of Jorge and Miss Venezuela seemed valid. And I was banking on luck and trust. "Mamá, if I can go, I can make money and see the world." She listened. "I really want to go."

She said, "I'll think about it. I'm going to call your dad."

I knew by her face that she didn't want me to move and that the decision was too big for her to make alone. She was concerned. But as I sat there that night thinking, I knew she'd let me go. I knew she knew I had to go and that I wasn't going to do the normal thing that everyone else did—school and work. I was aware of how much havoc I was causing us all, and I wondered if I would defy my mother if she said no. Then I banished that thought and came back to the idea that she knew me better than anyone on the planet, and that she was going to do the right thing for me after she'd thought it through, that she knew best what was right. I prepared myself for whatever decision she would make the next morning, but I was confident that her guidance would feel right. She knew I had a mission, and it wasn't going to happen in that building or city.

I fell asleep by the record player that night and woke up to the needle skipping. My mom was up early, and she came to me before she even got dressed for the day. She sat on the edge of my chair.

"If this is something you really want to do, go. I'm just going to ask you to be very careful. Europe is a very old continent. People are different. You grew up there, but you don't remember. And if anything happens, you come right back," she said. "Okay?" Her eyes were filled with tears, but she wasn't crying. I was so excited; I couldn't believe it. I called Jorge and he called the agency. They scheduled me to leave for Milan one month later.

That month I had a couple of obligations to fulfill before leaving, one being the pageant in Florida I'd been chosen for, which I was glad to make my last one, and some local obligations in Caracas. Two nights after receiving the news about Milan, I had to go to a cocktail party in Caracas for Miss Venezuela. There were going to be lots of important people there, including journalists and other famous Venezuelans. I arrived that morning and checked in to my hotel. I wasn't there more than an hour when the phone rang.

"Hello," I said.

"Patricia." I knew that voice. "It's Ernesto."

"How did you find me?" I asked.

"What, you're the only one who can track someone down in a hotel?" We laughed. "I called your apartment. Your sister told me. I'd like to see you. That is, of course, if you're not too famous now."

"Oh, you heard?"

"Heard? Are you kidding me? Of course. I'm so happy for you. I'm in Caracas for a few days," he said. He was playing in the band there for a big singer. "Then I'm heading back to Spain."

"Okay, I have an event tonight. Come. Does that work? Bring a friend if you like."

"Very much so, yes." I gave him the details for the party and hung up.

The tables had oddly turned. I hadn't so much as thought of this man in years, not since he had told me he had a girlfriend. But he had clearly thought of me. I was barely even intrigued about hearing from him. The excitement in my life, all that was happening, was more overwhelming than my teenage crush from years earlier. My life had changed so much too. I had become a woman. I looked different, felt different. I was the one in the public eye suddenly.

That night at the party, I recognized him immediately, but my reaction wasn't what it once had been. I saw him walking with his friend and thought to myself, *Hmm, he's old.* I didn't like him very much—or, rather, I was unimpressed. They approached and I introduced him to my friend, Monica. His friend and Monica, well, it was like the rest of the room didn't exist. The two of them just drifted away, clearly attracted to each other almost immediately. I was sort of caught up in the party. I'd never really wanted to be part of the pageant, but of course once everything happened the way it did, I was totally into it—the attention, the calls, knowing my life was right there in front of me for the taking. So while Ernesto tried really hard to impress me that night, and I could see in the way he looked at me that he wanted to, I just wasn't feeling it.

He was. At one point, he put his hand on my back and tried to pull me out of the fray for a private moment. I let him, moved by the tenderness in his eyes. I listened, though I had already checked out and was in Milan in my mind. I wasn't going to re-engage with Ernesto or any other man, mostly because I didn't want to get distracted from making money but also because I didn't want to get hurt again. Ernesto had, after all, broken my heart years before, and with my guard up more than ever, I wasn't sure I wanted to let anyone in ever again. He had rejected me, and that kind of hurt never really disappeared. But in the back of my mind I was thinking, *He'll be in Spain. That means I'll know one person there.* One person I could count on if I needed him. So I listened with my guard up, of course, but I heard what he had to say.

"So," he said. "I couldn't do anything with you back then, Patricia. You were so young, you know? I was trying to be respectful, but that didn't mean I didn't have feelings for you."

"I know. I've had time to think about it, and it's okay."

"And now?" he asked.

I paused and looked into my drink for a moment. "I'm heading to Italy soon. I fear our time has passed."

"Well, I understand. It's been too long, not that a day went by when you weren't in my thoughts. But just know that Italy is close to Spain. I will help you there if you ever need help. I want to."

"Maybe, yes. We'll see." My focus was elsewhere. I wasn't able to click with him right then and there.

We talked a little more that night, and our friends wound up hooking up, but Ernesto and I, after all the time that had passed and my desperation that day at the airport, did nothing more than share one kiss at the end of the evening. He escorted me to my hotel lobby, and we said our good-byes. As he was about to leave, he said, "It hasn't, you know."

"It hasn't what?"

"It hasn't passed. Our time."

And with that he left.

It was a confusing time for me—a mix of excitement about the unknown, fear of leaving, and sadness over the loss of a friend, as I never heard from Rossana. Despite my efforts, during that last month at home, Rossana never returned my calls. That was the most excruciating and horrible feeling, not being able to talk to her before I left. I felt excited about my future and sad at what I was leaving behind all at the same time. And desperate to hear her voice.

David was still in the picture. He'd done a really wonderful thing by sponsoring me and later, because he was a lawyer, he helped my mother prepare a case for divorce against my dad. It was funny, because we never knew life with my dad around all that much, so when they did finally divorce, the impact on us wasn't severe, though it probably was for my mother. I was indebted to David forever. Then there was Ernesto looming across the ocean when I arrived.

I didn't want to feel what I knew my mother had felt most of her life. I didn't want to be so enchanted by people, to have my journey so connected to theirs. It hurt too much. So while this blank slate and fresh start swirled in front of me, there were still all sorts of strands of my past spinning around as I left for Milan, hoping only for one thing: to take care of my mother and give back all that she'd given me.

Part Two

Chapter Ten

I lasted less than a week in Milan on my own before someone rescued me. Like so many times in my life, I should have given the city more of a chance instead of impulsively caving to my loneliness or leaping at the chance to live someone else's life. The modeling career was mine, but the control quickly became someone else's.

When I boarded the plane in Caracas, I hadn't anticipated how some men were going to behave toward me, starting from the moment Italian immigration hauled me in after an exhausting overnight flight. I landed, handed my passport over at passport control, and was immediately directed to a room where a few others were being questioned by Italian officials. It was hot under the fluorescent lights as I waited for them to stamp my passport, hoping to be on my way quickly. I was thirsty and tired from the flight, desperate to have a shower and see Europe again. But as hours passed and I grew increasingly uncomfortable detained in a plastic chair, I realized something was amiss. Through brief conversations with a couple of Italian officials, with broken English on both our parts, I got the hint: they wanted a date—or that's what they were calling what they wanted. I was being stalled and eyeballed and gawked at. I later learned that this was a common practice worldwide, particularly for models. After my fifth time telling one of these guys I couldn't see him that night, and their suggesting if I didn't meet them afterward they would send me back, I came up with an idea.

"Let me show you why I'm here," I said. Then I pulled out my sash and put it on. "I was in Miss Venezuela, you know? You can't send a Miss Venezuela finalist back, right?" I pieced those words together between Spanish and English as best I could. Whistles and catcalls ensued, but I stood there despite feeling humiliated. That was all it took. After eight hours of waiting, I was finally on my way. I knew instantly there would be an issue with men in Italy. I loved men, but this was clearly the most male-dominated culture I'd experienced, more so than even the Spanish one I'd grown up in.

I made my way to my assigned apartment, a large, dark place in Milan I would share with four other models—two English, one American, and one Polish. This was the first time I'd seen international girls or models outside of Miss Venezuela. They were so strangely, collectively white and pale that it was shocking to me. I showered and went to bed. My first appointment at my new modeling agency awaited me the next day. Lying in bed exhausted, a strange mixture of insecurity, excitement, and nerves enveloped me and I couldn't sleep. At home, the buzzing of air-conditioning often lulled me to sleep at night. The sound of silence in Italy, in that room that night, made sleeping a challenge. Then again, everything felt foreign to me, even the stirrings in my head about what I might experience the next day.

I entered a very old, gray, beautiful building, typical of Milan, and walked upstairs. On the outside it resembled old Europe, but once inside the office itself there was a dramatic contrast—youthful with modern furniture and people.

"I'm looking for Vittorio Zeviani," I said to the receptionist upon arrival. She was perfectly put together and polished, in a beautiful fitted suit and black pumps. Her shiny black hair was pulled back tightly, and her skin gleamed. The agency buzzed with people on the move, zipping from office to office and chatting and working and writing and talking on phones. It was alive and invigorating, and I marveled at the energy around me. The room had a hum to it. Being in the agency made things real for me. I waited in a velvet chair until the receptionist came to retrieve me. She walked me back to meet with Vittorio. He too was elegantly dressed, with perfectly shined black leather loafers and a gray suit that looked tailor-made for him. "*Ciao*," he said at first as I stood in front of him. "We're so happy to have you here."

He made me feel comfortable and welcome.

"*Grazie*," I said, then nervously added, "Thank you."

I knew so little English it was painful, but between Italian and Spanish and a few English words, one thing was clear: Vittorio, and by extension the agency, thought I was too big and needed to be skinnier. That, and they had arranged my first casting in Milan for later that same morning. I left the agency and checked my pocket map, feeling overwhelmed by it. I had to figure out how to get to the address they had given me, but it all looked so confusing. I took my time, took a deep breath, and when I finally sorted it out, I hopped on what appeared to be the correct bus. It took me two wrong buses, but I eventually boarded the right one. It felt like an accomplishment. I acknowledged my excitement as I spotted an empty seat toward the middle of the third bus that morning. I felt giddy with enthusiasm, smiling as I took it. This was the big leagues. I had made it to Milan, and I was on my way to an actual casting for a real agency.

The people on the streets were all impeccably dressed. I stared at them and thought, *How will I go about losing weight quickly in the coming weeks when I don't cook?* Jorge's chicken and tomato diet was an option. I hadn't even been seated for a few minutes when I was startled so severely that I jumped up out of my seat. The man next to me had placed his hand on my thigh, as if it was his right to do so. I stood the rest of the forty-five minutes to the casting in silence—and on guard.

Castings at any level were almost always the same, I learned. You walked in, someone looked you up and down, and they might snap a photo. This one was no different, except on my first casting ever I landed the job. That wouldn't always be the case for me. They instructed me to take the train to Verona in the morning for a shoot. Done. It only took the company—some catalogue—five minutes to decide that my face would work. I was jumping out of my skin with excitement. I wanted to call my mother and tell her, but of course that would cost far too much money, and I'd only just arrived. Smiling, I left the casting and wandered into the street. I found a small grocery store to get something to eat, knowing I would have to be strategic about my eating since I needed to lose weight quickly. I gathered some oranges and, still feeling somewhat frazzled from the bus ride, went immediately to the candy aisle. I saw something called a Twix bar. Judging from the picture, it had all my favorite ingredients: caramel, chocolate, and cookies. I bought one, stepped outside, unwrapped it, and took a bite. It was crunchy at first, and then it melted in my mouth. It was heaven. I was sad when I finished eating it. I decided right then that all I would eat, once a day, was a Twix bar. Forget chicken and tomatoes. Why not eat something I liked and, in doing so, reduce my calories enough to lose weight? I'd find some joy and solace—an escape from this overwhelmingly foreign world I was experiencing.

Back at the apartment that night, I decided before going on my all-Twix diet to juice the oranges I'd bought. I went into the big, bare, very European kitchen. It was white, but an old white—dirty white, not clean and new. With lots of tile. I found a knife and a cutting board. I sliced, but each orange I cut into was dark red inside. I stared at them all, thinking that this must be what happened when oranges spoiled. I tossed them one by one into the garbage, drank a glass of water, and got ready for bed disappointed.

Before I went to sleep, I decided to make a call. I pulled out Ernesto's number, called him, and let him know I was okay and in Milan. It was much less expensive to call within Europe than to South America, and there was one phone in the hallway for everyone on our floor to share. I wanted to hear a voice I recognized that was as close by as I could find. Using the phone card I had bought at a tobacco shop nearby, I dialed.

"*Hola,*" I said. "It's me, Patricia."

"I know your voice, love."

"I'm in Europe. Milan!" I said.

"I'm happy you're so close. How are you liking it?"

I didn't want Ernesto or anyone to know that I was already struggling with the culture and the men, and that I felt lonely and lost and like I didn't belong, though I suspected just a few words would give me away.

"Well, the oranges here are all rotten. I cut six in half and they had all turned dark red, so I threw them out."

Ernesto let out a loud laugh. "They're blood oranges. Have you never seen those?"

I felt stupid and naive. "Oh no. I thought they had gone bad. Well, other than that, everything is great."

Either sensing my struggle or just interested satisfying his own feelings, he immediately started pressuring me to pick up where we'd left off that night at the airport.

"Patricia, why don't you move here to Spain instead of staying there? Madrid is great. You'll like it," he said. I could hear the determination in his voice. I knew it wasn't about Spain; it was about him. He'd carried a torch for me—that had been clear the night I'd seen him after the pageant.

"Ernesto, I can't. I'm here to work. I'm not that young girl you met years ago. I am a woman now. I have a job in Milan. I'm going to work in Verona tomorrow, in fact. It's my first booking. It's very exciting," I said.

"You can work here in Madrid," he said.

"No, no. This agency, they chose me. I need to earn money—I have an agreement with them. I owe them for the trip here. Plus, I need to help my family. You must understand that."

A voice came on to tell me that the liras on my phone card were running out.

"I need to go."

"Okay, we'll—"

The phone disconnected on us. I wondered if Ernesto would keep trying to convince me to move to be with him.

The trams really made an impression on me. I could walk to a station, hop on, and disembark somewhere else. They transported me around the city and around the country if I needed. The trams pulled out of one place and pulled into another. It was something I had never experienced, and it amazed me. I also loved the sound of the trains, the noise they made as they moved across the tracks—the bells and beeps and doors opening.

Fresh off the first train out of Milan to Verona, I arrived for a photo shoot and was basically assaulted by the photographer the second I arrived. He had that long, loose Italian hair and dark skin, burned by the sun. He was aggressively groping me in between takes, and it took all my energy to pose, shove his hands away, push him off me when he rubbed up against me, and squeeze out of tight spots when he drew too close. I don't even remember how I felt about my first professional modeling gig because my thoughts that day were dominated by him and his horrible behavior. In a different era, in a different place, he might have been arrested for what he was doing to me. Still, I made it through the shoot, which was fortunately short, and emerged relatively unscathed.

My only escape while I was in Milan was my afternoon Twix, my one meal and my one source of peace. In just a couple of days I had grown devastatingly lonely, and I knew I had my work cut out for me. But I was determined not to complain to a single soul and certainly not to bail. I was sticking it out. I needed to send thirty dollars a month to pay for water for the building at home.

That evening I was walking back down the cobblestone street to my apartment after a day of castings. It was still light out, as it was spring heading into summer, and Milan was bustling downtown. But my street was off the beaten track and quiet. Europe to me, since I couldn't remember my very early years there, was different from home. It felt old in a way I hadn't expected, though perhaps I should have. Milan wasn't a particularly pretty city—the buildings had a dirty feel—but it had buzz. I came around the corner, sad that I'd eaten my sweet for the day. It wasn't enough. My stomach was growling and I had not lost any weight.

In front of the marble entry gate to my place stood Ernesto, leaning on a car. I stopped for a second, confused, then walked up to him. I didn't make a move to hug him or kiss him, but he slid away from the car and embraced me tightly. It felt nice. Comforting.

"How did you get here?" I asked.

He motioned to his car—a small, black, sporty two-seater. "I drove."

"I know that. I meant how did you find me? Know I lived here?"

He didn't answer. He just smiled.

"It's a long drive, no?" I asked.

"Yes, very long."

"Why?" I asked, though I knew. "And seriously, how? How did you track me down?"

"Well, I went to see Vittorio at your agency. You'd told me the name of the agency at some point. And I told him I would take you back to Spain and make you skinny. He said you needed to lose weight."

"Why did he tell you all this? I don't understand how you even found me."

"Phone calls. And I told him I was your boyfriend and that I was concerned," Ernesto said. "Aren't you happy to see me?"

I felt conflicted. I wasn't happy he was there, but at the same time I *was* happy he was there. It was a weird feeling, uncomfortable for me. I was excited about the support but wasn't sure I wanted him to be the one to provide it to me. I also wanted to live my life, the one I had come to live, not get swallowed up in his, which I felt was about to happen. Moreover, I couldn't believe how easily he'd tracked me down, and how uneasy I felt that the agency had told him not only where I lived, but also that I had to lose weight, as if his being the man in charge of my life made it okay.

"Look, I'm going to teach you how to eat. You'll be with me. You'll fly back and forth between Italy and Spain as you need to. This will work."

It was true that while the agency paid for my apartment, I had to pay it back out of earnings from jobs. That would be a savings. Plus, the apartment I was in, with girls I didn't really know or understand, felt hollow. It had no soul. None of us really understood each other, though I knew the language would improve in time. I wasn't there long enough to feel competitive, plus they all looked the same (and not like me), so we wouldn't have been vying for the same jobs. In Spain I would be able to understand the language, speak to people. Plus, Ernesto seemed to have it all conveniently worked out. I would fly to Milan for castings and jobs. I didn't even question him on it. He had all the information to prove he'd been through it all with the agency. It was so weird, but I just said, "Okay." I ran upstairs, packed my things, and climbed into his car. I gave it no thought, sort of like when I went to the airport to see him the first time. I didn't feel as overwhelmed or wowed by him, but I felt protected, and that was appealing at that moment.

We drove straight through to Barcelona, to a hotel where he was performing the next night. From the car, Barcelona looked and felt just like Milan, but bright and alive and pretty. The buildings were cleaner, not as gray and brown. Barcelona was vibrant—more leaves and flowers everywhere. With the window down, I was overwhelmed by the smell of the Plane trees.

While he was getting ready for his show in our small hotel room, my head was spinning. Sitting on the bed and staring out onto the city streets, I wondered if I'd made my own decision or if a decision had been made for me. I had known within a short period of time that I didn't like much about Milan. I knew being able to call someone my boyfriend would help me fend off people like the men in customs and on the bus. And I was just young and away from home. Plus, I couldn't deny that I felt flattered by Ernesto's cute gesture. Sensing that he liked me, I actually began to feel like it might be a sexy night when we finally had the time to make it so.

I didn't join him for the concert, but he kissed me passionately before he left. That was our first real kiss after all those years, and it was nice. Sweet. No fireworks, but special, the way I'd imagined it was supposed to be. And we had sex that night too—straightforward, gentle, tender sex. It wasn't experimental or crazy or lively, but just sex, which I also assumed was what it was supposed to be.

In the morning, lying next to me in bed, he said, "I love you, Patricia."

"I love you too," I said.

And I did love him, in my own way. I loved that I'd be taken care of and that he'd love me back. It was what I thought love was supposed to look like when I was growing up.

Chapter Eleven

I found Madrid so special because it became what Milan would never have been. A family finally emerged for me there within months—not blood family, but my friend Monica—who had hooked up with Ernesto's drummer friend back in Caracas at the party—had moved to Madrid too. She had a close circle of friends, and over time I became part of that inner circle, and we all supported each other. Not only was Ernesto taking care of me, but he was also introducing me to the world in a way I'd never imagined. He taught me how to eat and, as promised, put me on a diet. Without dance in my life, I had to learn to exercise for the sake of exercise. I hadn't had to do that before. Protein was the most critical addition to my diet. He had me eating red meat and taught me to cook. My favorite recipe, which I have continued to crave ever since, was a delicious red snapper with vinegar. He used flour, garlic, and salt. I found it completely mouthwatering. Most of my cooking skills, or at least the foundation for them, came from him.

Our favorite activity involved walking to this great old market, purchasing loads of fresh shrimp, taking them home, boiling and then chilling them, and sitting in front of the TV watching soccer and peeling shrimp. I found pleasure in this simple activity and in the intimacy that grew between us. I also grew thin, and that made the agency happy. I still had curves, Latina curves, but I developed a thin enough look to make it work. Sex was probably good, or good enough, though I'm not sure I ever fully enjoyed it. What I did enjoy was how much we laughed together when we hung out in his apartment, which was simple, nothing fancy, or when we went out and had fun. He had a tiny music studio set up in the apartment, and he spent a lot of time in there when he wasn't performing. I went to his concerts at night and started to learn the ropes of my work. At first it was very exciting. And then it wasn't.

There was increasing pressure on the relationship as my career began taking off, which happened quickly. I was flying with great frequency and, whenever possible, would make it home at night to ensure I was there with him, even if I worked a ten-hour day in another city. I was desperate for things not to fall apart between us, as I had grown to like the stability of having him around, but it was quite exhausting. What wasn't pleasant was the traveling—the back and forth to and from Milan for work. It had sounded like a great idea when Ernesto first proposed it, but it was a huge drain. I often had to stay in hostels with shared bathrooms, and when I finally started doing work in Madrid too, I had long bus and subway rides because Ernesto lived in a nice, but remote, suburb.

One night, I got in from Milan at about 11:00 p.m. (which was normal), and that was after flying there that morning on the first flight out at 6:00 a.m. I walked in and shouted Ernesto's name.

"Hello?" I yelled as I came up the stairs, down the long hallway at the entrance, and through the front door, dropping my keys in the little bowl I kept there. I knew Ernesto wasn't playing that night, so it was strange for him not to be home, especially when I'd gone to such lengths to get there to be with him. I changed, got ready for bed, and tried to stay awake. Lying in bed, I thought back and realized he'd been out with increasing frequency, playing less, but not showing up when I arrived home. For a few weeks, at least. I realized that the more I started growing and working and getting my own interests, the more we began drifting apart.

He eventually returned home that night, waking me at 3:00 a.m., wired and ready to talk. I noticed he was looking thinner than usual as he sat on the edge of the bed getting changed. I didn't say a word about it. I was tired and had to get up in a couple of hours to make another long trip the next day. But this had become a pattern: he worked less and less while I worked more and more. And I was certain he was using cocaine.

"What's happening with us?" I finally asked Ernesto one night when he had been out late but not working. "I feel like we're not so connected anymore."

He didn't answer immediately. He got up and stepped into the bathroom for a minute, then popped back out to respond. "Why don't you come to my concerts anymore or come out with me at night?" he asked. He didn't come close to me. He stayed in place, leaning against the doorframe.

"Well, I didn't know it was a problem or upsetting you until now, but also, I've gotta work."

"I know, but I want to see you more."

I wasn't sure what to say exactly. I was in town for short spurts. I came home when I could each night, to sleep in the same bed with him.

"Meet me tomorrow night. Please? I have a gig downtown."

I knew that meant getting off an airplane after a shoot, heading right to the bar, and staying out late. But I said yes. Clearly it had been bothering him, and the distance had been bothering me.

I met him there the following night, after landing back in Madrid from a day trip to Italy. I made it down the stairs into the smoky room with a red-light hue to it just in time to hear the last song. He was mesmerizing up there. I could see that. I felt young again listening, and I suspected onstage was the one place he felt young too. I was reminded of why I had been drawn to him initially. But he certainly didn't look like he used to. He looked gaunt and thinner—I hadn't noticed it so much at home, but he did.

He stepped off the stage, and I waved. He headed my way. "You made it," he said after a quick kiss that reminded me of my love for him and how much I cherished him. Then he led me by the hand to the bathroom, and we entered the stall together. We started kissing, away from the crowd. I wanted so badly to stay with this man. To make it work.

"Do you have any coke?" I asked. I felt determined in that moment to do what I needed to do to get closer to him, and I thought coke was the answer. I had never really been alone, and while I was beginning to gain confidence and feel secure professionally, I was worried he'd lost interest in me. He'd stopped smiling and joking, and it felt sad. I still felt I needed him in my life despite this. Maybe it was because I loved him, or felt what I thought was love, but maybe I was also afraid to be on my own and find out who I really was inside. I thought doing what he did would close the gap between us.

He was hesitant. He kissed me without answering.

I asked again. "Coke?"

"Are you sure?" he asked.

I nodded.

He pulled out a credit card and a little plastic pouch containing white powder. He poured it onto the back of the toilet, rolled up some money. Before he could stop me, I took the bill and did my first line of coke. It burned my nose. It burned my brains too. I could feel it absorbing into my body. I could taste it in my throat too—it was bitter. I was chatty immediately. I had energy, unexplainable energy.

He did a line too. And we kissed some more. I felt almost immediately like we were partners in crime. He didn't say it, but he looked conflicted, like he should have stopped me. But I think he knew he wouldn't have been able to. It seemed so desperate and so stupid. I hadn't done drugs before that. I knew it was wrong, but I didn't want to lose this guy and foolishly thought that doing coke would reconnect us. I wasn't sure we were unraveling, but I wasn't sure we were on a good road either. And we'd lost whatever had brought us together in the first place. I did what needed to be done to be close to him. I took my first line. We shared something, even if just cocaine.

"I want to hang out more," he said, suddenly kissing me furiously.

After that night, I went to bars with him as often as I could. I tried to be more stimulating for him and to do what he liked to do. The truth was that I grew to like the cocaine. A lot. It gave me so much energy, like I was alive, invincible, and in charge of my life. Powerful, like all was possible, like I could be anything. While it felt good, I knew it was the devil and poison, but it controlled me. It gave me a feeling I liked and made me aggressively pursue it as often as I could.

Chapter Twelve

While Milan was buzzing, Paris was the place to be. It was the fashion establishment. Paris didn't let anyone else dictate its trends—it set them. By the following year I was suddenly getting contacted by people to start working there. A small agency called Neo wanted to represent me. I was still desperate to be with Ernesto, so I kept my castings and work in Paris as day trips, just as I had with Milan. All the while, I continued using coke, pretending it was to keep the connection to Ernesto.

In addition to getting some traction in Paris, a significant break happened for me when Emporio Armani came to Spain to do a campaign. It was a big one and they were choosing one woman and one man to be the face of it all. Hundreds of models wanted this gig—everyone was talking about it—and at the casting in Spain everyone showed up to take a shot at landing it. A famous photographer named Aldo Fallai was there that day. I was paired up with a guy named Gonzalo for the casting, and after a few snaps with this photographer, we were both chosen right away. We were the only ones. Our faces would be everywhere. It was one of those life events that changed everything for me. But it also set the stage for my rock-bottom moment.

Gonzalo and I, along with a friend in the fashion business I'd met in Spain—a woman named Alicia—started spending a lot of time together, both working and not working. We did the Emporio Armani campaign and then ended up doing more work together in the months that followed. We all just hit it off and wound up on the road a lot together, and partying often in Madrid as well. The three of us used to hang out at this famous disco called Pacha.

Alicia was beautiful. She had enormous blue eyes and straight blond hair to her shoulders. Her skin was super tanned all the time. Her smile was captivating; she had very white teeth, the two front ones perfectly longer than the rest, almost rabbitlike. She was from the south of Spain, chatty and friendly. We would go to clubs and dance, but most people went to those places to get super high. I was no exception. My cocaine use had extended well beyond just using with Ernesto. Something else emerged from this campaign and my new friends: even though I made it home at night to be with Ernesto, for the first time I really started liking being out with my party friends and discovering the world on my own. I loved Ernesto, I did. But Gonzalo was this fabulous gay guy with endless energy and love for life, and Alicia—well, she and I clicked in the strangest way. I craved time with both of them. I just loved being around them. And they loved being around me too.

About a year into knowing them—when things were really starting to break for me professionally, when I felt I was truly building toward something important and significant career-wise—Gonzalo and I learned we'd landed a job together to do a shoot in Ibiza. A few nights before I was supposed to leave for the shoot, Ernesto and I made plans to have dinner with a girl who had come over from Venezuela to try to get work. She'd arranged to meet with me for some advice about modeling and living in Europe. Normally I wouldn't have shared my time with Ernesto, especially since I was leaving on a trip, but I had promised this girl we would connect.

Ernesto and I were sitting at a table having a drink when a girl with long dark hair, dark skin, and some curves approached. She introduced herself and sat down, and it was funny how much she looked like me. Her name was Maria. What wasn't funny was the shift in energy at the table. Ernesto's attention went from me to her almost instantly. She was peppering me with questions about modeling, and he was giddy about an otherwise trite conversation, every once in a while laughing a little too hard at what she had to say while she touched his arm a little too often. He and I had lost our connection, other than through our cocaine use, and he'd grown quiet in recent months, so to see him perk up like this in the presence of another woman was startling, not to mention upsetting and a blow to my heart. Still, after dinner I promised to help her find an apartment the next day, and then she went off to her hotel.

"Wow," I said to Ernesto as we walked down the dark, wet street away from the restaurant. "You liked her."

"I didn't like her."

"You were taken by her. I could feel it. You guys were totally flirting."

"No, no, no, no. You're crazy."

I spent the next day helping her get settled and the next night giving Ernesto the cold shoulder, which wasn't strange since we hadn't really been communicating too much anyway. It didn't matter, though. I was escaping for a night or two to Ibiza, leaving my cares in his apartment. I figured my stress would sort itself out while I was gone and that I'd deal with things when I returned. I didn't give Maria a second thought, and the pattern Ernesto and I had fallen into just seemed to be our life, so that was all fine.

Everyone loved Ibiza. It was a crazy place and a complete party atmosphere—vibrant, alive, a complete escape and release. There was nothing to take too seriously there—it smelled like the sea and felt sunny all the time. It was a glorious place. The client on this trip was El Corte Inglés—like the Macy's of Spain. They had this enormous setup at the beach during the day, and Gonzalo and I worked outside in the sun, changing between various outfits and setups for a long day. It was fun, in part because Gonzalo and I had grown to be such wonderful friends and working together was a blast, but also because I had grown to love the work I was doing. I loved expressing myself in front of the camera and getting that same joy I got from dancing. It was true that, at times, I stopped to think about what I was doing—that it was just, after all, selling clothing—but I realized more and more that fashion was art and expression and, most important, as a community, a safe and accepting environment. As soon as we wrapped that evening in Ibiza, we did a quick change, took off our makeup, and met up at a bar for a drink. I remember it was already dark by the time we arrived.

Everyone from Madrid hung out in Ibiza in August. The bar where we'd started our night was packed with people ready to get crazy. For some reason, whether it was the era, or the freedom I'd come into, or my confidence, everyone just seemed fabulous. Some of the crew from the shoot swung by, and we soaked up the wild energy that flowed in the summer.

After a drink or two Gonzalo made a head gesture, and I followed him to the bathroom. We crammed into a stall, which was hip—even the bathrooms in Ibiza were hip—and did a line. On the way out, feeling sexy and alive, we bumped into a dealer we recognized. We'd met him in Madrid many times before.

"Hello," he said. He had long, curly hair and was really tall.

"Hey," I said. Gonzalo and I both intended to get really high. We didn't have to ask this guy; he knew. We bought coke from him.

I realized he was on crutches. "What happened there?"

"A little trip. Fracture," he said, brushing it off. We weren't yelling, but the music was loud.

I wanted to do coke because it made me feel invincible. Gonzalo was one of those perfectly gorgeous gay men. He made me feel like a million bucks all the time. By that time, too, I'd come to the realization that people thought I was attractive, though I still didn't think so myself. So partying together that night, we received a lot of attention. The coke made everything seem just gorgeous and great, and the music felt beautiful, and we felt beautiful. There were no bad thoughts.

Gonzalo noticed how much cocaine I had bought. It was a lot.

"We're already fucked up, Patricia," Gonzalo said.

"But it's Ibiza, and we're having so much fun!" I said. Everyone else looked so happy, and I was high and not being smart. Gonzalo agreed. We did more coke, and then we were just talking and talking. It was like we couldn't stop talking and promising the world to everyone. We were yammering on about nothing with anyone and everyone and making the rounds to talk to other happy people. It was an unstoppable high. Every once in a while, I'd feel the urge for more and grab the dealer guy, and go into the bathroom to do more.

Before I knew it, and I don't remember how or where or any timeline, I was at this dealer's home on the water, just hanging out. It was beautiful. He didn't want to have sex with me; he just wanted to keep partying. Gonzalo and I did too. We were up all night. By 7:00 a.m. I said, "Holy shit, we've gotta go. We've gotta check out of the hotel."

The dealer guy said, "Stay here for the weekend. We'll keep partying."

We were way too messed up to get on an airplane at that point, but with no cell phones at that time, we thought we'd better at least go tell everyone traveling with us what we were doing. Someone with a convertible drove us to our hotel because we knew the crew was waiting for us to catch our plane back to Madrid. We pulled up, music blaring, laughing, and poured ourselves onto the curb. The two of us, still in whatever we'd been wearing the day before, came flying into the hotel, a little disheveled and loud in the otherwise quiet lobby. The crew was there with bags and cases. We were still high as kites.

"We're staying!" we announced loudly, with more energy than we should have had at that time of morning.

A couple of people asked if we were sure and if we should just go. We said we wanted to stay. Everyone else was going home. The shoot was over.

The stylist tried to convince us. "You guys are messed up—you should not stay. Come on, go home. Go home."

I said, "No, no, no, we're having fun. We'll go back tomorrow. It's not a big deal. We already did the job."

We went back to our new best friend's house and did more coke. We were really messed up. We sat around and talked nonsense, thinking we were having the most intelligent conversation of a lifetime. Once our noses started burning too much, we stopped taking it. My nose was even bleeding. I waited until I felt I was straightened up enough to call Ernesto. I went into a quiet room in this guy's place and dialed. It was getting dark, but I had no idea of the time or even what day it was.

"Hey," I said. "We just finished up the shoot. Later than expected."

"I've been trying to reach you since yesterday." He might have known I lied, or he might have known I was high. I didn't care at the time. "The agency has been looking for you. Call them."

I probably should have felt more panicked, but I didn't. I chatted with him for a few more minutes and then hung up and called the agency. Chantel was my booker at the time.

"Hello," I said. "How are you?"

"Good, Patricia. Where have you been?" Chantel asked. "I've been trying to get you."

"I'm in Ibiza." She obviously knew that; she had booked me. "We were having fun so we decided to stay. I'm at a friend's house right now on the beach. It's so beautiful."

"Patricia, I can't believe this. We've been working for this so long. We got a call this morning from *Telva*. They called last minute, and they wanted you for the cover."

Telva was a major fashion magazine. I had never done a cover that big before. This was everything I'd been working toward, and I was thrilled I'd finally landed it. "Great! Where and when?" I asked.

There was a brief silence on the other end. I shifted in my seat, gripping the phone tighter.

"We couldn't find you," Chantel said. "You just lost the job. I'm sorry. They needed an answer ASAP."

I was so fucked up, and my head was about to explode.

"Oh, no, no, I can't believe it. Can't we get it back?" I insisted we could.

"No, Patricia. We can't. You know how this stuff works. You have to be quick with these things. People cancel at the last second, and whoever on their list answers the phone first gets it. Why would you stay and party? You can't do that. Look, we've been working toward this for a long time. Get it together."

"Chantel, we can get this back. How can we?"

"It's over. We can't. It was very last minute, and they needed you by now." She hung up. It was a disappointment to her too because she'd been working on landing me a cover for a long time. That was the goal. That was why we did everything we did—to get a cover.

I ran outside and found Gonzalo watching the sun setting. "You're not going to believe what happened." I told him what I'd missed. I felt so much guilt and like such a failure, and a complete loser. His reaction said everything. He looked crushed for me and probably for himself too. We wanted the same things. Plus, though I'd made my own decisions, I could see he felt guilty for being my partner in crime.

I walked over to the water and sat alone to think. I couldn't even cry. A year of coke had dried my tears. It was the weirdest thing, feeling that sadness and torment, which would usually cause the flow of tears, but then nothing would come out of my eyes. *What am I doing? What have I done?* I knew I wanted to hide from something, some feelings, some lies, but I hadn't really stopped for long enough to think about it until that moment. I just kept numbing myself with more and more. That cover would have changed my life. It could have provided so much for my mother. I had failed. I'd worked toward one thing and let it slip by being an idiot. I was so ashamed of myself and my behavior, it was overwhelming. I vowed then and there never to do another drug for as long as I lived. I'd missed the opportunity of a lifetime, and I was determined to work my butt off to make a second one for myself. I also knew it was time to start figuring out some truths about myself, where the hole was that needed filling and why I'd let myself linger in an unknown longing for so long. I needed to get my life together. It was time.

Chapter Thirteen

Japan was as foreign a land as I could have imagined and a place I had never anticipated visiting. I couldn't read a sign or understand a word anyone said; the streets were buzzing and electric, and everyone smoked as they hustled from place to place. Getting to Europe was certainly a huge deal for me, but Tokyo was unimaginable. When I was contacted by a woman there named Tateoka, I couldn't believe my good fortune. Not only was I about to travel there, but also I was about to receive a lesson in humanity and kindness. I was also about to be given a chance to redeem myself after my horrible behavior in Ibiza. The way Japan worked in the modeling world was that an agency would get you there, and you'd have one week to go to multiple castings. If you could land five or more jobs in that one week, then you were allowed to stay in Japan and work and be paid an enormous amount of money for your stint there, which at the time was somewhere between $16,000 and $20,000.

I flew to Tokyo shortly after the Ibiza debacle, and the morning after I arrived, I was put in a van with half a dozen other models, along with a representative from the agency, Tateoka Models. I remember the motion sickness I felt in this hot, crowded van, holding back gags as we crawled through busy Tokyo traffic. The Japanese were efficient with time; they really used the clock there. It was impressive. They didn't book things in fifteen-minute increments. They would have appointments at, say, 1:37 or 3:22. Down to the minute. As such, we'd be paraded in front of maybe twenty clients a day, all of us hoping to land a magazine, catalogue, or whatever was available. So there we were, crammed in our van. It would pull up, and we'd file out and head into a room. Not that I could have spoken the language, but like most castings, you didn't talk. You didn't wear makeup or get too dolled up because the goal was to look natural. You just walked into a room where a bunch of men and women would look at you, nodding and discussing as they flipped through your book and your agent spoke for you. You sat and stood as directed and then climbed back in the van for the next stop.

At this time, which was early 1991, the entire modeling world was still predominantly white; that was apparent in any country and on any continent. I was not considered exotic, as that concept hadn't really been defined. I was dark, and the divide was basically blonde and everything else—black, Latin, Asian. We were all grouped into one category. In Japan, it was a vanload of white people and me. There was a really cool Canadian girl named Amy making the rounds with me that week and a girl from Spain. Obviously, I'd connected with the girl from Spain, mostly thanks to ease of communication. She told me her mother had died blow-drying her hair while standing on a wet floor. That conversation struck me hard and created a lifelong fear of blow-dryers that never went away.

At the end of the week, after all the castings, we were called into a room to meet with the woman who ran the agency, one person at a time. I sat in the lobby with the other girls, waiting for my meeting. It was an austere room—minimalist in its decor. My stomach had butterflies. As the door to the office opened and my Spanish friend left, my name was called. We passed each other as she came out, and with a shake of her head, I realized she was not staying on to work.

I took a seat in front of Tateoka's desk. She was so tiny and put together, and we could barely communicate with our language barrier, but she said to me, "Clients like you. You stay. Next week you work." That was it. I sat longer to hear more but realized that was all there was to know. I had been hired. I was going to have some real money in my pocket in a few months. My Canadian friend received the same good news, and everyone else was sent home. I was sad to see my Spanish friend leave, though, as I would soon learn, making friends in the modeling business was difficult. I was on my own and on the move, and there was little time for much else. Over the next few weeks, I realized the clients took to me because I had a slightly Asian look, or maybe because I brought a new look to modeling. Whatever it was, I worked like crazy.

I admired the Japanese culture and the people's sense of honor.

Everyone took pride in what they did, and there was a strong sense of community. Like in Italy, the clubs tried to attract the models by offering us free dinner. Models were just starting to get that rock-star status, so the club owners wanted us around. We were a draw. I wanted to save every penny I was earning, so wasting it on food wasn't an option. You had to be smart or you'd spend what you earned and have nothing to send home. In Italy it was bordering on prostitution to go to these clubs for the food, as you had to accept a lot of groping to eat for free. Eventually, after six weeks or so, it got a little old in Japan too, and while I wasn't groped, I was constantly turning down advances. Ironically, the clubs served no Japanese food. They were smart enough to serve burgers, chicken, and more international dishes to draw us in. They knew what kind of food we were craving.

One night in Japan, a guy approached me three times, saying, "You pretty, you hot. You come with me." Some girls would have. They were desperate. I wasn't. Many of these girls were new to traveling and didn't have any guidance. It was sad to watch and an even sadder reality that some girls weren't brought over to model but instead were lured by fake agencies, tricked, and then put to work as sex slaves. This practice occurred all over the world, not just in Japan. It was a tragic reality of the business. This one night, I eventually had to push away this guy to get away from him, and, having watched what other girls were accepting, I decided that this would be my last free club meal. It was raining and dark as I ran out of the club that night and found a taxi, which I knew would be expensive. While it was nearly impossible to communicate because of the language barrier, if I was trying to get somewhere and needed directions, adding an "o" to the end of left or right—saying "lefto" or "righto"—would get me farther. I discovered that on the cab ride home that night out of necessity.

By two months into my stay, I had learned to get around the country on my own. I'd started taking the subway and using the high-speed trains. I'd grown more comfortable with the culture and its differences. One morning after returning from Osaka, Tateoka called. She asked me to come to the agency and meet with her right away. The streets on the walk over from the subway were crowded as usual. While navigating the crowds, I tried to replay in my head whether something had gone wrong that week with a client, or if maybe she'd heard about the incident in the club, which made no sense to me. No one else knew about that night or my experience. It was terrifying. Tateoka had not called me in randomly like that before. When I walked in, I was stressed that I wouldn't see my money for my time there. The sight of her distracted me because her hair was so big, for a Japanese woman. She was sitting behind her desk with her oddly wavy hair.

"Sit," she said, nodding.

I did.

"We pay you today. In yen. All your money. Okay?"

I was stunned for a second. That wasn't what I was expecting to hear. "Okay, but why?" I wasn't sure if I was being fired or paid out or what. She quickly explained that something dramatic was about to happen in the currency or stock market, or had just happened; I couldn't be sure. And that if she paid me my $16,000 then, with the exchange, if I changed it over immediately, it would be worth nearly double.

Tears welled up in my eyes. Here was this woman, running a tiny but significant agency with just five models, and she was doing me a favor, giving me a gift really, by paying out my contract in advance so I could take advantage of a currency boom. It was an enormous gesture on her part and really special to me. It was probably the single kindest gesture I'd ever witnessed. She had no need or reason to help me. It didn't benefit her in the least. But it showed me there, and I'd see it again later, that there were women in the modeling world—tremendously powerful women—who genuinely cared about the well-being of the women who worked for them. It was an indication of the collective strength of women and the power of caring. It was a wonderful and enlightening gesture that stayed with me forever.

"I can still stay and work?" I asked, knowing I had more jobs still in the works.

"Yes. I pay you all now though."

My urge to hug her surprised me, but surprised her more when I actually did it. It was a formal culture.

I went back to my apartment, and the next morning, knowing it was nighttime at home, I made an expensive phone call to my mother to tell her everything had paid off—all the suffering and hard work she'd done to raise us. I was going to wire money when it landed. That money, along with the proceeds from the sale of her apartment on the hill (which only happened because my brother Juan hustled to get it sold on very short notice), was enough to buy her a new apartment in a nice neighborhood away from the old place. If that had been it—if that had been where my career ended—it would have been enough. I had finally moved my mother into a new home. My family wouldn't struggle like it had been. I'd done it.

Chapter Fourteen

As much of a success as Japan had been, Madrid remained somewhat of a failure for me. My relationship with Ernesto had seriously deteriorated. I had stopped using cocaine, and so had Gonzalo. We both vowed to live healthier lives. It was fair to say that my financial victory was short-lived, as I was still hiding out from the truth to a degree, not yet having told my family, after almost two years, that I was living with a man. As they say, misery loves company: When my brother Fernando called to say that he too was struggling in Venezuela, I suggested he come for a visit. We were all worried about Fernando because he'd desperately wanted to work in the aviation wing of the military. He'd been accepted into a prestigious school to do so—which was an accomplishment—but a year in, he didn't pass the very last exam that was required and therefore couldn't continue. He was distraught and devastated.

I'd desperately wanted to share my life in Europe with someone and was happy Fernando was joining me. It was good to pluck him out of his environment, as he had a tendency to get into trouble there, plus it gave me the chance to put some of my crap on the table for him to hear. That was liberating. My life in Europe had remained a mystery to my family back home. My feelings of being lost and lonely, and my living with a man out of wedlock, remained a secret. Not that it compared to the lie I'd eventually live.

When I went to meet him at the airport to take him back to my apartment, I told him what he'd find out within the hour.

"Fernando," I said on our train back to Ernesto's apartment. "So, I have a boyfriend here."

"That's great. When did you meet him?"

"Well, technically five years ago. But we started dating two years ago."

"Two years, Patricia, and you don't tell anybody at home? Why the big secret?"

"He's a bit older, I guess, and I wanted to make sure everybody knew I was working hard over here."

"Oh, we knew. The apartment and the money. You did a lot to help Mamá out. She's very grateful. We're all grateful. So, will I meet this guy at some point on the visit? This boyfriend?"

"Well, of course. Because we live together." I was worried that detail would put Fernando ever the edge. He was a traditionalist, and in our culture, Catholic girls didn't live with men until they were married.

"Patricia," Fernando said loudly before looking around and lowering his voice since we were sitting in a train. "How long have you lived with him?" he asked.

"Two years," I said.

He looked worried. "Don't tell Mamá."

I didn't say anything. There was nothing to say. My actions had been wrong, both what I'd been doing and the fact that I was lying about it. And that upset me. We rode the rest of the way in silence. He was pensive while I panicked. Lying killed me, but the disappointment my brother felt toward me was even worse. I couldn't let anyone else in my family know.

Fernando gave Ernesto a chance that first night. He was open-minded. I introduced them to each other at home, and the three of us went out for a great traditional Spanish seafood dinner. But the next evening something shifted. Maybe Fernando had time to think or assess, because something was in the air. When we returned home from a day of touring Madrid, Ernesto wasn't there. He had gone out to perform. Maybe to avoid any immediate discomfort and to distract Fernando from what I sensed he might be feeling, I made a plan for us.

"Fernando, let's go out." I just wanted to get away. The tension with Ernesto had grown, and having Fernando there gave me strength to face it. He made me feel protected, my big brother. I wanted to just be with him and draw from what he was there to offer.

"You'll love Madrid at night," I told him as we got ready to head back out. I didn't want to address anything else right then.

We took a cab to a cool club in Chueca, the gay neighborhood of

Madrid. We couldn't hear what music was playing, but we could feel its beat out on the sidewalk. I grabbed Fernando's hand and we went in, down a steep set of stairs and onto a dark dance floor. We laughed a lot, but he sensed things weren't right at home for me, so he was quiet the entire night. His older brother instinct had kicked in, and he was worried. We danced and we laughed and we stayed out for hours, but there was a weight on the night. I hid what I was feeling. But he sensed my worry. When we got home, Ernesto still wasn't there. He should have been because it was at least 2:00 a.m. I couldn't hide being upset from Fernando when we came home to an empty apartment.

"Well, where is he?" he asked as we made up the couch.

"I'm not sure. He should have been home by now." I paced a little across the living room, with my arms crossed, while my brother just watched. Finally I said, "Let's just go to sleep."

We did, and when we woke up Ernesto was there, but he'd been out most of the night and must have rolled in as the sun came up. Fernando and I were having coffee when Ernesto stumbled into the kitchen. Neither had much to say to the other. There was a nod of acknowledgement and a chilly "Good morning."

"Where did you go last night?" I asked to break the uncomfortable silence.

Ernesto didn't answer right away. Then he said after a long pause, "I met some friends. We had drinks."

"Oh, you could have come met up with us. Where did you go?"

"Can't remember the name of the place," he said, his back to me as he looked out the window over the kitchen sink. My brother ever so slightly shook his head, more to himself than for me to see. He was not impressed. The chill in the room was palpable.

My brother never said anything, but I knew he didn't like Ernesto, and I knew Ernesto was up to something. I just felt it. Fernando said he was heading out for a quick walk. He wanted to give Ernesto and me some time alone, as we hadn't really had any.

Without hesitation I asked, "Are you cheating?" This time he didn't look out the window, he didn't lie, nothing. He just sat down at the little table in the kitchen beside me and said, "Yes."

"You're sleeping with the girl from Venezuela, Maria, aren't you?" I just knew it was her. And if I was right, that meant it had been going on for a long time already, maybe months.

"Yes," he said. And he seemed almost relieved he'd been caught and that the lying was over for him.

"I'll move out as soon as I can," I said.

He just nodded.

And that was it. There was no screaming, no fighting—it was all calm. But cheating was so horrible to me and cut so deeply. I don't think Ernesto even wanted to be with me in those last few months, but he wasn't able to get out or was too weak to say so himself. I'd been traveling so much and staying in Paris more and more, and it just wasn't there between us anymore.

Later that day I found a hotel apartment in downtown Madrid, and my brother and I packed up and went to stay there. It was a miserable little place and expensive despite its modesty. I was insanely upset, even though part of me knew Ernesto wasn't more than a safety net for me. Still, I was beside myself at the relationship having ended. No tears would flow still because of the coke. The pain existed, however. Emptiness overwhelmed me, like I wanted to cry, but nothing would come out. The feelings were there but not the tears. It was the strangest sensation—being devastated but tearless.

The timing, it turned out, was almost perfect. As the relationship with Ernesto ended, something else big happened in my life. Within a couple of weeks, a new opportunity presented itself.

Chapter Fifteen

Neo Agency had asked me several times to come to Paris permanently while I worked in Madrid. We'd done work together, but moving there didn't feel like the right choice, mostly because my relationship with Ernesto had been hanging on by a thread and I wasn't ready to let go. Just before my brother arrived, I'd finally landed a cover despite the Ibiza mishap. It was for *Ragazza* magazine, whose director, the woman in charge, eventually went on to head up *Elle*. Her name was Susana.

We shot it in Cuba. That was the furthest I'd ever traveled for one shoot. That cover was plastered everywhere—huge billboards and bus stops all over the country had my face larger than life. In the photo, I had a blue bandana on my head, the sky was blue, the ocean was blue. It was a striking image. Around that time Neo had begun pressing me even harder, asking me to join them in Paris. While my *Ragazza* photo was still up on all the billboards, a woman named Iris Minier from Ford Models came to town. I was told later that Iris had left a casting she'd been on, and while she was sitting in her car, she saw the poster of me from Cuba on a walkway. She went agency to agency to track me down until she finally found mine, insisting on meeting me. She hit a stumbling block: my agency refused to make the connection, but she didn't take "no" for an answer. It was a surprising and enlightening phone call that changed my life. I was at home in our little hotel apartment one night when the phone rang.

"Hello, Patricia?"

"Yes, hello," I said.

"My name is Iris." She was speaking Spanish. She told me she had grown up in New York but was from the Dominican Republic. "I'm from Ford Models. I scout models, and I'm here in Madrid. I'd like to meet with you right away, as I'm only here until tomorrow."

"Should we connect through my agency?" I asked. That was protocol.

"No, no. I tried. They wouldn't put me on with you or even set up a meeting with them. I had to ask some girls who knew you, and I finally found someone who did. That's why I'm calling you at home. Your agency is doing something you won't like. I want to talk to you privately. Just meet me."

I did. At the Hotel Wellington in Madrid, wearing, I remember, a one-piece jumpsuit and my black boots. Iris, who was tiny, with a round, bright face, big teeth, and a great smile, was sweet. Pretty, cute, and younger than I had expected. She wasted no time and no words. Ford wanted me in Paris with them. She was direct and to the point, and she explained straight out that the agency wouldn't connect me to her because they'd promised me to another solid agency in Paris. I was outraged that my agent was not putting all my opportunities in front of me. The agency, it seemed, was making deals that were mostly in their best interest, and so a lot of backroom horse trading had occurred. I was angry.

In addition to just trusting her because she'd been so honest, I hit it off with Iris immediately, and she became one of the single most important and influential women in my life, like a sister to me, over the years. I was thrilled she was with Ford, of course, but it didn't matter. I would have gone with her no matter whom she worked for.

"Listen," she said as we sipped coffee in the hotel lobby, "you're striking. Ford has never really been known as the agency that has exotic girls. It will be a challenge and a lot of hard work, but I think you have what it takes."

"I'll sit at the back of the bus, Iris, to work for Ford. That's fine. I'll fight my way through the blonde standard. The fact that you want me to go to Paris when you're up and running is a dream."

"We need time, but we'll get you there."

"Neo has called many times," I said.

"Patricia, go with them for now. Get to Paris. I'll let them know that you'll work for them for six months or whatever, but that you'll eventually come to us once we are fully operational."

That night I told Fernando what was offered, that I was probably going to move to Paris.

"This apartment is gross. I've spent enough time in Spain. I think it's time," I said.

He looked sad, defeated almost.

"What's wrong?" I asked.

"I've enjoyed spending this time with you. I don't want to go back to Venezuela."

I looked at him and said, "So don't."

"Can I move with you? Can we move together to Paris?"

"I don't see why not."

I called Neo and said I would like to go to Paris, but on one condition: if they would move both Fernando and me there together. They said they would, and we were off to start something new. Together.

Chapter Sixteen

The agency issued us an apartment in the Latin Quarter in a little pocket of the city close to St. Germain called St. Michel. It was rough, with a constant, overpowering smell of shawarma, but I loved being there anyway. I loved the vibe and Paris and being with my brother. We lived on one of those tiny little side streets on the first floor of a small, old building with a very Parisian entry—a giant blue steel gate that led to a courtyard and our front door. The most startling aspect was that the place had no windows, except one small one facing the alley in the kitchen; and therefore no light. If you wanted to know the weather, you had to open the front door and step out. It was cute enough inside, and Fernando and I were so thrilled to be in Paris that anything would have excited us. He felt comfortable and seemed to love it immediately. Seeing Fernando happy filled me with joy, and at the same time, I felt freer than ever being away from Ernesto. From the moment we landed, we were smiling, and that smile stayed with us.

My two other brothers, Carlos and Juan, were academics and basically brilliant, and because my dad was so focused on education, he probably favored them growing up over Fernando, who had other skills that exceeded all of ours. He just didn't receive the same opportunities. A big scholarship took my two older brothers to Mexico to study after high school, but they stopped giving those scholarships out when it was Fernando's turn, and from there he just never really found his stride. He seemed to sink lower and lower, struggling to get something going after that. His gift was that he could fix anything. If the record player broke, he was on it. He could pull anything apart and reassemble it quickly. Fernando also had this funny way of sleeping as a kid; I remember he would hang half off the bed and half on, and he was a sleepwalker. I had sleepwalked too, and once in a hotel I wound up on the wrong floor, trying to get into the wrong room. In Paris he slept soundly. And to see him smile and look comfortable and at ease was the greatest feeling. It made me think there was hope for us all.

Because we had little money, Fernando and I would walk everywhere from our little apartment. The benefit, which I hadn't yet experienced in my career, was having someone to accompany me to every single casting. We would stop off at the agency each morning to retrieve the list of castings, I'd carry my book with me to show my previous shoots, and then the two of us would travel from place to place on the subway, the bus, or by foot. Fernando would wait outside each stop for me. I only had two outfits suitable for castings, nothing designer at that point, and I had zero money to upgrade. We walked so much that we both had holes in the only pairs of boots we each owned. We also ate the same meal every day, which was the cheapest food available: McDonalds from the Avenue des Champs-Élysées. I walked for so many hours that eating fast food once a day didn't matter. Fernando had planned to stay for only a month, but at the end of the month he loved it so much he asked if he could remain in France with me. He studied French and I worked. Ernesto was a distant memory.

One morning when the weather was particularly miserable, Fernando and I stepped out our front door to find it was freezing cold and raining. Within just a few steps, the water had leaked into the holes in our boots. Within an hour, we were in trouble.

"My feet are freezing," I said to Fernando.

"I know. I can hardly walk," he replied. Our umbrellas, already in rough shape and on their last legs, were blowing open with the wind. It was hard to keep it together and look presentable at the castings on that day's list, and by the last couple, we were almost hobbling, our feet were so cold. We made it through the day, but by the next morning we were both sick.

We huddled over hot coffee in the kitchen, and Fernando made us both eggs. "That's it. Let's go to the flea market. We need new shoes," I said.

"It's too much money, Patricia."

"We have to. This is ridiculous."

There was steady enough work and money was coming in, but between sending it home and repaying Neo for the costs of our home, I wasn't getting ahead. It was the normal course of modeling at that stage, and at that time things were okay—good, in fact—but I had no cash to spare. That morning, sick and between castings, I bought us new boots at the flea market that resembled the black ones we were wearing as closely as possible. While I loved my work, the strain of it all began to weigh on me for the first time—the early mornings, the back-to-back appointments, the lightless apartment, the language barrier, the holes in the boots, the attitude of the Parisians, and the damn shawarma smell. For some reason, that morning it just came down on me heavily. I felt weighed down and questioned what I was doing and whether I was getting anywhere. I wasn't depressed, but I felt defeated. That night, as we sat there doing some math, figuring out what was left for the month to spend and feeling sick and deflated, something wonderful happened. Ford called. Four months into my time in France, Iris invited me to her apartment to talk. The agency had officially opened in Paris.

Chapter Seventeen

Iris, Fernando, and I had grown very close in Paris, even before Ford opened. She took care of us there. It felt like family. We'd often spend weekends at her beautiful apartment in front of the Centre Pompidou museum. It was in a square and had a special little terrace. We'd sit out there on a Saturday or Sunday and smoke cigarettes, drink wine, and eat grilled vegetables and meat that Iris would prepare for us. And we'd talk and talk about everything and nothing. In Spanish too, which was such a treat because I was still struggling with my English, and while I'd grown up speaking French, it just hadn't clicked back in for me. She was the greatest company, and perhaps because of the language, being with her just felt like home—maybe culturally somewhat too. This one particular weekend, with news of Ford, we talked a lot about getting ready.

"We need to prepare your look," she said, flipping the beef with verve. She was spirited, both tough and soft, and lively. "I want you to remember, Ford is very much about being natural. Don't wear high heels, especially those Latin ones, and just keep your clothing simple."

I loved when Iris was all business. I soaked it up like I was at university, listening, studying, learning everything I could from her.

"Be nice on castings, which I know you are, and don't say much. Just be you."

"This is so exciting!" I said.

"Oh, we'll move you into a new apartment too," she said.

I looked at Fernando. We couldn't contain our enthusiasm. We laughed out loud, we were so thrilled. We'd long outgrown what had once felt charming in our apartment.

I completed my time with Neo, so that afternoon at Iris's place we celebrated. Neo was understanding about getting me there and gracious about letting me go. Ford was it, the top shelf, the place to be, and I was on my way. Elite had already set up in Paris, and Wilhelmina too. But Ford, it was something.

"Katie will be here next week. She's running things now," Iris explained. "You'll need to meet her."

I didn't laugh or respond. I just kept thinking, *Oh my God. I'm going to meet Katie Ford.*

The Ford offices were massive, modern but French, their impressiveness and significance magnified by the fact they were at Place de la Concorde on 242 Rue de Rivoli. It was so dramatic and grand. As I walked up a few exterior steps and pulled open a massive door, I was reminded that I was in the big leagues by the real estate alone: a long, long hallway with high paneled ceilings stretched out before me. Impeccably dressed people moved around, quickly, but barely filled the expansive set of offices. As I was taking it all in, I heard Iris's voice off to the right. There, between a set of white double doors, she sat behind an elegant oak desk.

"Patty, come in here."

As always, Fernando was with me. He didn't immediately move when she called for me. He was staring up at the ceiling.

"This place. It's so big," he said before snapping to. "I'll wait out here in the lobby. Go."

I walked into Iris's office, but she stepped out from behind the desk and said, "C'mon. I'll take you around."

We walked out into the hallway and into another enormous open space, off to the side with a large table. I met a few people, including a woman named Domitille, who was going to be my agent. She had a thick French accent and was buttoned-up and elegant. We immediately clicked.

"Welcome," she said. "We are going to get you right to work. You'll have castings tomorrow."

I nodded and looked at Iris for a little help with the translation. English was the fashion world's language. I was working on learning it, but I had a long way to go. I didn't feel embarrassed or awkward either; Iris was clearly in charge at Ford, so while the people I met that day were great, it was extra special because I was with Iris and I liked my agent immediately. That was all that mattered. And it was Ford. Ford!

As we walked back to Iris's office after a few short meetings and many hellos, Iris said, "Okay, let's go meet Katie."

"Is she here?" I asked.

"No. She's at the hotel." We said good-bye to Fernando and headed off to meet Katie Ford.

We drove to Place des Vosges to the Pavillon de la Reine hotel. Like everything in Paris, it was beautiful too—one beautiful building after another. We went up a few flights in a glitteringly lavish elevator and entered a set of double doors. The French seemed to love their double doors. The suite had a staircase in it. A hotel room with a staircase! It was cozy and grand at the same time, which hit me because grand things are usually cold, but this was not; it was warm.

Iris and I sat on the couch and waited. Katie, tall and lean, with fine features and wavy, soft, light brown hair, came down the stairs with her little two-year-old daughter, Alessandra, ahead of her. Once they reached the floor, Katie moved swiftly about the room. I stood, and she gave me a kiss on each cheek and a hug. Then I sat back down again.

We had a little chat, but Katie didn't sit still the entire time. Yet she still focused her light, hazel-ish eyes on me. She paid attention to and engaged in our conversation, but she moved around, signing papers on the desk, organizing objects on the floor, and playing with Alessandra as well, while we became acquainted. Even though she flitted around, she appeared incredibly relaxed, and I marveled at her grace. She looked American to me, like what I would have imagined a New Yorker might look like. She wore jeans and a blue summer shirt—casual but sophisticated, and not what I had expected. She was one of those women who didn't need to wear makeup. Her smile lit up her face, and she was beautiful. She was also beautiful on the inside—kind and friendly, soft and approachable. Like a mom. But she was Katie-freaking-Ford. She talked fast, like a New Yorker—I could tell that even without English in my toolkit—but she came across as warm and genuine. I learned to read things about people as I traveled because I often didn't have language in common with them. Katie exuded a profound sense of caring and being on top of things. Oddly, we understood each other too. Immediately. It was just a feeling, like we got each other. She was fascinated by Venezuela and the culture, as she'd traveled there often, and we talked a lot about that. With Iris translating and Katie dipping into a little French and some Spanish, I learned that Katie's plan for me was to build up my profile in Paris and then get to New York—the place to be once you've made it in fashion. The place to make money. New York City.

"Patricia," Katie said, "we're going to build your career here. When you're ready, we'll get you to New York." I was encouraged to hear her say that. Girls who looked like me weren't considered big in New York quite yet, so for her to suggest I could get to New York was really a risk and bold for her agency full of light-skinned models.

Life, it was becoming clear to me, was made up of moments and people, and this series of connections, some more significant than others. That meeting that day with Katie Ford was one for the books. She was one of maybe five people who changed the course of my life and became a friend forever. One moment with one of the most influential women in fashion and I felt so clear and positive. Iris had prepped me in the car on the way over by telling me that the Fords were selective, but once you were in, you were forever part of the Ford family. I felt that the second we met. I had found a second family and a place where, for the first time in a long time, I felt a sense of belonging and did not feel like an outsider. When I left, I remember walking away feeling on top of the world.

Chapter Eighteen

Marie Claire Bis was a huge deal in France. It released twice a year and was almost as important as Italian *Vogue*, but with less advertising. It had tons of fashion shots. Each of the two issues would sit on the shelves at the magazine stores for six months, which is why everyone wanted to be a part of it. Every photographer wanted to shoot for it, and models wanted to be in it.

I received a call from Ford saying I'd be going on a shoot for *Marie Claire Bis*, arranged by an influential Japanese stylist named Macu. Along with an important Swiss photographer named Christian Moser, who had a strong Swiss German accent, we were sent to a country in West Central Africa—one of the poorest countries in the world, Benin. I did considerable research once I heard I got the job. I had always been fascinated by the Yoruba religion as the origin for voodoo and white magic. All those practices come from Benin. It was deeply ingrained in the culture there. That kind of spiritual thinking was rooted in my culture too.

After a long flight into a tiny airport, we had to drive to where we were going to shoot. A guy was waiting for us at the airport with a van, and since the government had arranged everything, they chose a really special and remote place for us to shoot. But we were already exhausted beyond belief from the flight. The van and the driving made us weary and shot. We kept asking, "Are we there?" or "Are we close?" This driver kept responding, "Just a bit more. Just a bit more." It was made even more tedious because the scenery never really changed. It was the same and the same and the same: red clay, dusty and sparse, but with a surprising amount of greenery. Dirt stretched out ahead of us for miles and miles.

Finally, maybe six hours in, Macu snapped in front of us all—the makeup artist, photographer, everyone—and started fighting with the driver. It was sort of funny to watch her fighting in French with a Japanese accent with a guy speaking French with his Benin accent.

"Where are we going?" she demanded from the very back seat. "Where are you taking us?"

In later years, a trip like this would have required that we travel with security, but not back then. So it was weird and somewhat worrisome that we had blindly hopped into a random van and allowed ourselves to be taken so deep into a foreign land none of us could find our way out of if we ever needed to.

The driver repeated himself. "Just a little bit more."

Six hours later (for a total of twelve!), we arrived at our destination. It wasn't really a dangerous country. The town we were in was super small. We stayed in a tiny hotel with only four or five rooms in the middle of a village that had maybe two thousand people. Mostly scientists went there—anthropologists who wanted to study and do research. I slept a lot; we all did. The next day I spent some time exploring the town. What I found most unique as I sat out in front of my rugged little inn watching the comings and goings of the population was that people shared belongings. There were a few bikes for communal use in the middle of the little town. People would use the bikes and then return them when they were finished. If you needed a bike, you used it. You shared it so you could get where you wanted to go. In Venezuela this would never have happened. People would never have returned them. The bikes would have been stolen for sure.

I remember sitting out there watching this form of sharing and thinking, *Wow. This is so great that this thing can happen, that no one is stealing.* I found it amusing that something so simple and right seemed so foreign. As I watched the town activity from a little bench in front of my hotel, I thought about my research. If I drew a line around the globe, at the same latitude from the town in Africa, it would hit Venezuela. We were on the same parallel. And yet so different. The dirt in Benin was so red and less dry than back home. I was intrigued as well by the spirituality of the region and how it was a part of me—the foundation of my people too. It all made me think of home—my indigenous roots, my mom, my culture. A feeling of homesickness surged through me in that moment, and despite the places I'd traveled, a place like Benin reminded me where I was from, what I was made of. A sense of pride swelled inside me. Understanding my roots was part of being from Venezuela, a place I loved and missed.

The night before one of the shoots, the hairstylist, Lucia, did my hair. She wanted to prep me for the next day by rolling my hair in toilet paper rolls to sleep in so it would have lots of volume by morning. That was one of her tricks. I knew I was in for something big and exotic. The next morning he finished up, and my hair was gigantic. We drove a short distance to a beautiful waterfall. It was like a string, this waterfall, maybe running as long as twelve to fifteen feet, only from top to bottom. Not quite what everyone had expected, but we had to make it work because that was our planned location for the day. So while they were setting up, I wandered off, which is something I've done my entire life, perhaps because I'm indigenous. I made my way around and up to the top of the waterfall, to see where the water originated. I was standing up there when, out of nowhere, I was surrounded by natives—seven or eight strikingly beautiful, tall men. Their skin was very black. They were dressed in loincloths, and they immediately started yelling at me. I was so in awe of how gorgeous they looked that it took a second for the fear to set in. I couldn't tell what they were saying or what language they were speaking, but their anger toward me was apparent by their pitch; they were almost screaming. Vulnerable, away from my team and worried for my life, I just stood there frozen. Suddenly our driver appeared and said, "Whoa, whoa, whoa—they're speaking the local language."

He then spoke to these guys somehow, negotiating and fighting with them. They all just turned around and left.

He grabbed me. "We've got to leave. You can't be up here."

"Why not?" I asked.

"We have to go down. We cannot be here. There is a spirit on these grounds. It's private."

Had he seen me climb up to this sacred, protected area, maybe he would have stopped me. My heart was beating quickly as I began to climb back down. I was scared and knew they wanted me out, so I tried to move fast.

The shoot turned out to be amazing, and I remembered it so vividly, maybe more so than any other shoot. That night we sat down to dinner at the same little rustic place in the hotel we'd eaten a few nights before. On Monday the waiter said, "We have chicken and rice." The next night, beef. The next, pork, and by Thursday we had pasta. Then on the final night he said, "You can have anything you want from the week."

We were all sitting around this little table outside, and it was hot. We realized they had just saved each meal from earlier in the week to serve us leftovers. So I said, "I'll have what we had yesterday to be safe."

The people there were poor. Extremely poor. They lived in these little adobe homes made with a collection of towers with thatched roofs— almost fablelike. In one we visited, the cattle slept downstairs and upstairs slept the mother, father, and boys and girls. We shot outside there by a big fire one evening. It was magical.

The magic continued. Weeks later, the same magazine called back for a second shoot with another one of the greatest photographers in the world, Paolo Roversi, leaving me feeling dumbstruck. I'd shot with Christian Moser and now was getting a chance with another legendary photographer for one of the most important magazines in the world at the time.

———

"Hi, Patricia," Iris said into the phone one morning, a few months after the *Marie Claire Bis* shoot. "What are you doing tonight? Come over for dinner. I have a surprise for you."

"What's the surprise?" I asked.

"I'll tell you when you get here. Freddy is coming too. We'll have fun."

Freddy was an American gay guy whom Iris had befriended.

"Bring Fernando," she said.

"He met a girl. He's out with her tonight."

Iris had piqued my curiosity with talk of the surprise, but after a busy day working, it had all but been forgotten that night. Freddy greeted me at the door. I was barely one step into the apartment when Iris scurried out of the kitchen, beaming.

"Congratulations. You just made it!" she said.

"Made what?" I gave her a confused look.

She walked over to her desk, picked up a magazine, and handed it to me. It was summer's *Marie Claire Bis*, and the photo from Benin was on the cover, featuring me in a simple white linen dress with white espadrilles that tied up over opaque black tights. My hand was in the air, as if I was dancing. Dance and my ability to move were going to be my secret weapons—that much was clear from the photo. Using the skills I'd learned in dance would help me stand out on my shoots. Despite our differences, I was grateful in that moment for all I'd learned from my early dance teacher, Soraya. Not simply to pose, but to make each pose a dance step for each click of the camera, moving my body like I did during dance, giving my hands energy—that would stand out in photos. The cover was the start of that strategy, that energy, and using my skills as a dancer my secret weapon. During shoots I would dance in my head so that the right energy flowed. It wouldn't be about being beautiful or exotic but about using dance to make a mark.

"So," Iris asked, "are you excited?"

I was speechless. With my mouth hanging open, I shook my head slightly, flipping through the pages and then coming back to the cover in amazement. That cover equaled possibility. Real opportunity could follow. It meant I was for a moment entitled to be doing what I was doing. I deserved the work, something I had questioned on almost a daily basis. I had felt like a poser at times, as if I was invading someone else's world. But this cover meant it wasn't a fluke or good luck. Maybe I actually had *it*. Maybe my lifetime of hard work and paying my dues had led to this moment. That cover was the payoff. It meant that I could accept the payoff for my efforts. I could receive that moment. It was a turning point.

"Do you want to call your mom?" Iris asked.

"It's too much money," I said. "No, no."

"Call," she said. "It's okay."

It was all I wanted to do. Iris handed me the receiver.

"Mamá, I've got to talk very fast because this is expensive. I went to Africa on a shoot, and I got on a cover of a very important magazine."

Explaining to her that it was one of *the* most important magazines in fashion was difficult since she didn't know that world, but she could gather from my enthusiasm that it was significant.

"I'm so happy that you're happy," she said.

She must have known it was important because I was choked up. And I never cried in front of my mother.

Chapter Nineteen

Our new apartment was spacious and had tons of light. The girl Fernando had met occupied a lot of his time, so I saw him with much less frequency than when we had first arrived in Paris. Instead of having him around to talk to in the morning, I listened to the TV. Getting ready for my casting calls one morning, the TV was blaring a French station. The background noise comforted me, especially when I was alone, even though I didn't speak French. I could hear the TV from the bathroom, which was this odd green color. Staring in the mirror, brushing my teeth, I turned off the water. At the same time, some story on the news caught my attention. Watching the TV backward in the mirror, I learned there had been a small accident. Although no one was hurt, the police were looking into it. I spun around and looked directly at the TV, toothbrush still in my mouth. I could suddenly understand every single word they were saying. In French. It was as though I had trained the muscle in my head to understand French when I was a little kid, and suddenly it started working again for me. My ability to listen—maybe not my vocabulary or full-fledged ability to speak—had magically returned to me, like a light switch.

Something else clicked around that time too. The number of jobs coming my way picked up. Many were small ones, such as catalogues and small magazines, but every job was equally important to me and I was grateful for every project. Plus, I was earning a little more money to sustain myself. I felt like I was on fire.

That morning at the agency, my agent gave me my paperwork for the day. First stop: Karl Lagerfeld. I reread it a couple of times. Then, standing there holding the paper with my mouth open, I looked up at her and asked, "Karl Lagerfeld?"

She wasn't as moved or shocked; she barely even looked up. "He wants to get into photography."

"Like, become a photographer?"

She nodded.

I left, walked directly to the address given, and entered the studio he was using. It was dark and minimalist, but large. There were some lights, a stool or two, and some equipment. An elegant man with a white ponytail all dressed in black had seven assistants working around him to get set up. This wasn't a normal call. This wasn't a fashion stop. Karl was designing for iconic houses—Chanel, Chloé, Fendi, and Lagerfeld. He was a legend.

"Hi, darling," he said in a thick German accent as he approached me. He asked my name and where I was from.

"Oh, Venezuela," he said. "I love Venezuela. I love your country."

Smiling, I tried to communicate with my limited English. Then, with little fanfare, he had me stand in a specific place against a black backdrop. His assistant didn't adjust anything or let him know things were lit correctly, which would have been standard on these sorts of shoots. It was just a simple setup. Despite the simplicity of the setup, I felt the grandness of the way he worked. This was Karl Lagerfeld—the man with more presence than anyone in the industry. He was *it*. In French, he informed his assistants that he was ready to begin. I never revealed to people that I could understand French or Italian, not that morning, because I wasn't confident enough in my new discovery. I didn't reveal it later either. It became my secret weapon—hearing what people were saying without their knowing it. I got tired of not knowing what was being said in Japan or Germany, for example, so I listened in when I could, continuing to pretend.

Once ready, Karl snapped a few shots. He adjusted me a bit and put me on a high stool. Click, click, click and we were done. "Okay, darling, thank you." Kiss, kiss.

That night I washed some clothes in our washing machine, which was still a bit of a novelty. Prior to living in this apartment, we had washed everything by hand. The machine was that very slow, European kind that both washed and dried (though nothing ever got dry) in one machine and took hours to complete one load. I only had a couple of shirts and one navy blue leotard bodysuit with thin spaghetti straps that I wore all the time. I was hanging them outside to dry when my brother returned home. I told him I'd met Karl Lagerfeld.

"Well, what happened? What is he doing with the photos?" he asked.

"I don't know if he's doing anything. I'm just not sure. I think it was just a test."

The phone rang, and Fernando ran inside to answer it. He called me over and I ran in, my hands still a bit wet.

It was my agent. "You got the job with Karl Lagerfeld."

"What? Wow."

"It's tomorrow. Write down this address. It's at seven a.m."

I had barely hung up when Iris called to congratulate me too.

"What do I do?" I asked. "I'm nervous."

"No, no, Patty," Iris said. "Just show up. Like any job. Just be yourself. He seems to have liked you very much."

"Maybe because I'm Venezuelan?" I asked.

"I told you, you are going to be the one to make the change and bring that exotic look into the world."

The next day the agency told me it was for the cover of a small but widely read magazine. It was going to be big because it was his first photograph and his first cover. The shoot was in the same place we'd met the day before, but this time modern music blared from the speakers. Julien was there to style my hair. He was a very crunchy French guy, but there was such easiness about him as he worked. As we shot, I remember having a feeling that I would experience over and over later in my career: that we were all artists in the room, doing that shoot. It made me realize life offered many possibilities. I also felt a connection to my days as a dancer, belonging, as if nothing else existed—feeling present 100 percent of the time in my work.

Just the chance to work with Karl Lagerfeld was crazy to imagine. He would take a photo, then come and touch me, adjust me. Always quickly, then he'd snap away. He grabbed a set of pearls, strung them on me, and had me hold them in a few ways, and when I made it to the place he wanted me to be, he said, "Okay, good, good, good, good, good, okay." It all happened quite fast. When we were finished I handed the pearls back to him.

"These remind me of my mother," I said. "She loves pearls."

"Where's your mother, Venezuela?' he asked.

"Yes, she's coming to visit soon."

We chatted briefly for a couple of minutes. I took off my makeup, fixed my hair, and stepped outside. The day had surpassed anything I could have imagined, and I felt sad it was over. Deeply sad. When I arrived home that night, Fernando, his new girlfriend, and some friends of ours were all waiting.

"What's wrong?" he asked. "You have such a long face."

"I'm just bummed it's over. It was so great. I feel sad. I just want to go to sleep."

"No, no, Patricia. This is a celebration. Let's go have some fun."

We did, but it was the weirdest sensation. They were all excited, and I too was happy about the day, but having it end had made me feel lost in a way I couldn't understand. We purchased some wine and cooked dinner, and then we all headed out to the Eiffel Tower, which was right across the street. We had a nice time, but inside of me emptiness swirled. To make things worse, my brother told me that night he was going to move in with his girlfriend, Heike. She was German, and her father, who was very wealthy, had bought her a really big place. I was going to be living alone for the first time—that meant living with myself and my thoughts alone. Who was I? What did I want? Excitement and worry washed over me all at the same time, as no distractions meant confronting something weird I'd started feeling. Something I didn't quite understand.

Once my brother started living with Heike, there was no need for the two-bedroom apartment anymore. Ford found me a bright little studio apartment on Avenue de Suffren. It had so much light and good energy. It made me feel like an adult, my independence somehow represented in that home, a glimpse into being grown-up and on my own. To compensate for Fernando's absence and my feelings of loneliness, I kicked my work into high gear. Fernando, Heike and I hung out together at Iris's house on weekends. Things were going well for me; the Karl Lagerfeld photo had been pivotal. But something was still missing in my life. I didn't know what, exactly; I just felt a void.

My brother came by my apartment one night, alone, which was strange, because he and his girlfriend were usually inseparable. When he walked through the doorway, he looked distraught.

"Sit down. You want some wine?"

"No, I don't." He sat. "We're breaking up. It's over," he blurted it out.

They'd been together for more than a year.

"Why?" I asked, giving him a hug. He didn't get up. I just reached down as he sat. "Why, Fernando?"

He didn't speak immediately. Then he said, "Her dad doesn't like me. He's holding all the money. So, it makes sense that he'd have that power."

"But that's always been the case. What's different now?" There had to be more to it; that was evident. We sat in silence for a bit. I didn't want to press too hard, so I let him get to it when he was ready.

It poured out and there were many small reasons and many big ones, but ultimately it was over. My take was that he'd pushed Heike away for some reason, and then she broke up with him, probably with some pressure from her father. What was he going to do with a guy like Fernando, who had no real status and no real job? Worse, after he'd been doing so well, studying at Alliance Française and loving Paris, he was leaving. He felt it was time to return home to Venezuela, which proved to be the best thing that could ever have happened because he met his wife there. But for me it was a bittersweet time. I cried; my tears had finally returned now that I no longer used cocaine. Maybe I cried a bit more than the situation warranted. Maybe being able to cry again was a good thing. Either way, I was scared. I was truly going to be alone. I'd lost the one person who'd really accompanied me and been by my side. It was having to learn things about myself I'd ignored that was terrifying.

Chapter Twenty

Even though I was sad my brother had left, I had begun to exude a completely different but refreshing energy after the Lagerfeld shoot. Maybe it was simply taking care of myself, but whatever it was, it seemed to land me some new and exciting work—primarily, a runway show. The first fashion show that I walked in was for Comme des Garçons in 1992. It was a very important show put on by a well-respected group of Japanese at the Louvre in Paris. Getting ready that morning made me feel more nervous than I'd ever been—about to walk with Linda Evangelista, Christy Turlington, and Tatjana Patitz, just to name a few of the models who would be there that day. I'd neither met them nor worked alongside that caliber of model. It was scary and unfamiliar. Plus, the Louvre was intimidating because it was one of the world's most famous museums. On the runway we were about to become part of the art—like live sculptures.

Smoking a lot of cigarettes and drinking a lot of coffee that morning helped me through my panic. I couldn't eat. I showered, and even though they told me not to wear any makeup or have my hair done, I considered as I stared in the mirror with a cigarette in hand whether I should put on a little bit of base. I decided I shouldn't. But then I did, then immediately washed it off. I blow-dried my hair super straight and plain, even though I knew they'd redo it when I arrived. Just before I left, I ran back in and put just a dab of base back on. Just to be safe.

A taxi seemed a wise choice, both because I was so nervous and because it felt far too early in the morning to depend on the subway. The call time was 6:00 a.m., and I didn't want to risk being one second late. It was still dark as I walked across the cobblestone street toward the entrance, taking in the beauty of the museum and all its grandeur, lit so perfectly by the rising sun. There were tons of people walking in as well, which on any other day wouldn't have been the case at that hour, but on this day it required a large staff to put on a show. I had to act calm, but the thought that *This is the Louvre!* kept running through my head as I walked by them.

Even though I'd begun to grasp French, I felt a little embarrassed about my English, and I didn't want to look like that crazy foreign person who spoke broken English, so I tried to look like I knew what I was doing. Weaving my way to the big white tent set up for the show, I entered a big sectioned-off area with racks and racks of clothing lined up every-where, lights dimly lit, and people running around working, setting up everything. The hair and makeup people were set off to the right side against the wall. Everyone was dressed in black. Everyone. Hair dryers were buzzing all around, and models were walking in too. It was exciting and intimidating all at once. I stood frozen for a minute, unsure of what to do, before spotting Julien d'Ys from the Lagerfeld shoot, relieved to know someone.

"Sit here, sit here," Julien said when he saw me. It was his show. He was the star in charge of all the other stylists. So when he said, "I'll do your hair," it made me feel safe and a little bit protected

Scanning the room, it became apparent the really big models hadn't arrived yet. Apparently, the bigger you are, the later you show, the tighter you push it until show time. I knew the show started at 9:00 a.m., but I wasn't taking any chances. Jockeying for the head stylist was part of the backstage hustle. Not an assistant, not the second best—you wanted, at that time, to be in Julien's chair, a reward for being ultra-early. My hair was eight inches high by the time he finished. It was enormous and awesome. Makeup was next, and within forty-five minutes my look had been transformed. Super early, of course, but ready. I took the extra time to look for the stage entrance, which was close to makeup, and then I wanted to find my clothing. Names were attached to each of the racks. Walking up and down each row, not daring to ask anyone for any direc-tion about what was supposed to happen, I saw a couple of the bigger models start to arrive and head to makeup. Nadja Auermann was first, the German girl. She was mesmerizing.

At one point, the intense loud laughter of two people cut through the rest of the buzz, ringing out above the music and the hair dryers. I thought to myself, *They are American.* Their English conversation was loud. I pretended to ignore them, but I was observing them while I went about my business. Not that he was a remotely familiar face to me, but there was André Leon Talley, of *Vogue.* He was a titan and had a commanding presence—big, black, very gay, and flamboyant. It was impressive that he could be so open and be what he wanted to be. In the world of modeling, everyone was accepted. It was different from the world in which I'd grown up. I had an epiphany about fashion right there and then: This is fashion. This is acceptance. Everyone from all over the world just coming together to create. The woman André was talking to was unique looking. She was tall, but tiny somehow next to him, and had chin-length curly hair and a large, wide brightly lipsticked mouth. She didn't look like a typical model, though she was very pretty. Comme des Garçons used other types of girls in the shows because they believed in all types of beauty. This woman's movements were feminine, and she had such a nice look to her. Warm. As she was talking to André, I passed by and she stopped suddenly mid-sentence, looking directly into my eyes.

"Hi," she said.

There was silence.

Then I said, "Hi," and kept walking. It was sort of weird and shocking, yet I was oddly drawn to the warmth of the exchange. It was almost confusing to me, but I wasn't sure why. I felt like a little bird, lost and out of place, so I kept moving quickly to find my name, afraid to stop, for fear of revealing myself as a poser.

Seeing my name on a rack of clothing, along with my Polaroids, was such a special moment that I gasped. I looked around to share the moment with someone, but the rows of racks were empty. Suddenly, unsure of what to do, I just sat down on the floor by my clothes. Quiet, terrified. Everyone else was smoking and drinking champagne, talking to each other. Not me. I sat by my rack—guarding it with my life. It made me feel safe to keep it in my sight as I waited to be dressed. Being a professional meant staying where I was until someone dressed me, which made me think of my mom. What would she tell me to do? She would say, "Patricia, be quiet and respectful." The Japanese were quiet and respectful—that much I had learned from my time there. I thought, *They'll appreciate my efforts if I behave well.* So that's what I did for an hour and a half until someone came to dress me: pretended to read but actually took it all in, looking around, capturing the moment in my head like a series of snapshots to remember forever. André's laughter was still echoing throughout the room.

Linda walked in eventually with a handler. She was so beautiful and perfect that it was almost startling—modern in her jacket and high heels, and larger than life. She went over to talk to André, greeting him with a double-air-cheek kiss. I could hear "dahling" this and "dahling" that, and I could see the woman who had said hi looking at me every once in a while as she spoke to them. I pretended not to notice.

When Christy walked in, suddenly, between seeing her and Linda and how beautiful they both were, a small panic attack set in. What was I doing there? I didn't fit in. I didn't look like these girls. I wasn't nearly as elegant. I wasn't even remotely as pretty and not even close to being as tall as they were. I was overwhelmed by it all and felt water swell in my eyes. Just then, the woman André had been speaking to was beside me. She startled me, as I hadn't even seen her approach. She kneeled down beside me, and immediately my tears retreated.

She touched my arm and said, "Hi. I'm Sandra." She must have felt my angst. "What's your name?"

"I'm Patricia," I said.

"Nice to meet you."

"Nice to meet you too," I said.

"You're nervous," she said. She hadn't moved her hand from my arm. It felt warm and comforting.

I nodded.

"It's okay. It will be fun, and it will be okay." That's about all I could make out. She kept talking and I nodded like I knew, but I didn't have a clue what she was saying.

"I don't speak English," I said every once in a while.

But she just kept talking. With every word she said, I just felt less lonely. Plus, she knew something about me I didn't even know about myself. Something I'd learn later.

Within minutes of that encounter, it was hustle time and two Japanese dressers started dressing me. I was the first to get ready, it seemed, and I was very careful, dressing very slowly to get everything right. My first outfit was loose and drapey. Other people started getting ready too, but they were a little bolder. They were taking off their clothing, standing there naked, and getting dressed. I shielded myself somewhat because it felt uncomfortable to do otherwise. It was a habit I never really shook over the years.

I was startled out of that thought by the voice of the producer. It was show time.

"Okay, Nadja, Linda, Christy . . . Patricia . . ."

Everyone was drinking champagne until the second they stepped out. There was someone waiting, taking glasses almost at the curtain. At that point you just went. Everyone started coming in and walking through the curtains one by one into the lights and the crowd. Marianne Faithfull was blaring from the speakers when I stepped out. It was nothing short of electric. It was clear in that moment that this was all I ever wanted to do. I was born for that stage. A sea of photographers snapped and flashed, all compressed in a group. All we could see were the flashes. It was empowering in part because I was there, and also because I knew the singer had come back from some bad drug-use experiences too. It felt easy, and even though I was different, hippier, more Latin, and knew that I'd never be a part of the club, so to speak, I was going to own my work. Also, I wanted whoever bought what I modeled to feel they were part of the experience. During that show I decided to accept myself. That was going to be my strength going forward too. It was a great show and was over in what felt like seconds. I was hooked. I was free.

When the rush and excitement died down, the music stopped and the breakdown backstage began. I hoped to find the woman I'd met and thank her. There was a bit of commotion—the press had been let in, and they went straight toward her. I had absolutely no idea who this woman was, but they clearly did, and they wanted to talk to her. She went with them to another area and gave me a wave as she did. "I'll check up on you," she said as she was hustled away.

I learned later that these shows sometimes did stunts and brought celebrities in to do a walk. Still, it seemed weird that they wanted to talk to her, not Christy or Linda.

I returned my final outfit and donned my street clothes. Eventually the curly-haired woman made her way over to me.

"How did it go?" she asked.

"Great," I said beaming.

We were all being hustled out because they had immediately started to wrap things up and break down the stage, but she walked with me as I moved through the chaos.

"I wanted to thank you, but all those people," I said.

"Don't pay any attention to that. Listen," she said. "I have to fly to London at four o'clock. Can we get together now or before I go? I want to see you."

"Yeah, I'd like that. I have a casting now. Later maybe?"

"Yes. My name is Sandra Bernhard. I'm at the Hotel Montalembert. Why don't you come over and visit when you're done? I'll wait."

We agreed and both left. I was so excited I'd met my first real friend. I hadn't made many new friends in Paris, just friends of Iris or my brother. This was a first. It was exciting to think about having someone new to talk to. I ran into a coffee shop to brush out my hair and take off my makeup, grabbed a café latte, and left. Like always, once the last remnants of the show were washed away, that feeling of emptiness started. On the subway I thought, *Maybe a friend will help me beat this feeling, and I won't be lonely each time a project ends.* Then panic hit. *Oh my God. I have no idea the name of the hotel she gave me.* I got off at Champs-Élysées and climbed the stairs, trying so hard to remember what she had said. My enthusiasm turned to anger. I felt angry about not having learned enough English, just angry and foolish. *Why didn't you write it down?* I had blown my chance at having a friend. I was fighting with myself in my head the entire way to the casting, surprised at how furious the incident had made me. Once at Publicis, an agency, I took the elevator up and sat down in the lobby. My head was spinning—in part replaying the show and what I'd just done and in part being angry at myself for forgetting the name of the hotel. And her name? Not even her name stuck with me, which made me wonder why seeing her seemed to have meant so much to me.

A woman working at the office interrupted my thoughts.

"Patricia," she said in French as she approached, "you have a phone call."

I stared at her for a second. "Me? Here?"

"Yes."

Who could be calling me? Who knew I was there? Maybe the agency.

"Hi," I said into the receiver.

I knew her voice. It made me smile.

"You forgot the hotel, right?"

"Yes." I was ashamed.

"Ask someone for paper." I did. "Write this down."

I did and told her that I'd meet her there after my fitting.

"How did you find me?" I asked.

"I called your agent." Not that I minded in this case, but these people certainly were free about giving out information about me. She must have been very famous to get them to talk, because in France they wouldn't give that information out, not like in Italy. Not like when Ernesto basically convinced them to let him take me to another country. Ford was much more protective of us.

Time couldn't pass quickly enough during the appointment. I was dying to see my new friend. My mother had taught me never to show up anywhere empty-handed, so after the fitting had finally finished, I stopped at a typical French bakery and bought pastries. Once at the hotel, a romantic-looking building, I headed to the top floor as directed. There was very little time because, as she had said earlier, she was leaving for London shortly.

Without a word, I handed her the box of sweets and then we started talking, not about anything serious, just simple pleasantries. Short sentences. Basic words so I could somewhat understand her. Out of nowhere, she started gently touching my arm, rubbing her finger back and forth. Softly and slowly. I had no idea what was going on, or what to even think of what was happening, but I didn't reject it. I liked it.

I didn't immediately understand what was transpiring. It was almost an out-of-body experience at that moment, like a movie playing in my head. Within seconds a lot became clear in my life. I suddenly looked back and gained some clarity on some women from my past. My first thought was of Alicia, of how my love of being her friend was maybe something else, something more. Something forbidden. Alicia was really the only person I had kind of tried to do something with but didn't end up going through with it. Looking back, that was definitely a crush. She'd had a crush on me too. She was a Gemini. At the time she loved coke too. I was so attracted to her, but so confused that, once in Tarifa while we stayed in a little white hotel, in two tiny twin beds, we had our moment that I'd forgotten until now in Sandra's room. That summer with Alicia was full of crazy energy, as was often the case in Europe. I opened the door to our room late one night. She said, "Shut the door." She was hunched in the dark, looking out at the water. I was confused but joined her anyway. We could see tons of little flashlights moving. We were on the southernmost point of Spain, so we watched out the window as all these little lights scurried about. She explained that it was drug trafficking, bringing in hash to the country from Morocco. After we watched the action by the water, Alicia lay down. She invited me into her bed by opening her sheet to me. I didn't get in. Nothing happened. We had to go. I said, "We've gotta go. We've gotta head back to Madrid." We never talked about it.

Nothing. It just passed.

Lost in so many moments at once, I looked at Sandra in front of me. Then I thought of holding Rossana's hand—that wasn't just friendly. It was more, but I had resisted. I'd resisted it all, confused and uncomfortable with what I'd felt all those years. This time, with Sandra, I did not resist. What she was doing, the way she was touching me: that would never go over at home. Women were touched by men, not other women. This was forbidden, and I panicked that my family would somehow know my innermost feelings, and they would shun me and think I was a failure.

I casually stepped away, just far back enough for Sandra not to be touching me. But she stepped forward and put her lips on mine. Once, short at first, and then boldly again, and we kissed while standing there. It was soft and short. I'd never kissed a girl. It was softer than kissing a man. More tender.

Then it was over. "I have to go to the airport," she said. "Can I come back and see you tomorrow?"

My head was spinning. I didn't know what to say. She was waiting for an answer, but I wasn't giving one. I had to go to another fitting, and I needed to think. We said good-bye and I ran out toward the elevator. I hit the button, waited, and then ran back to her door and knocked. She opened it and I stepped in.

She hugged me tightly; I didn't really hug her back. I wasn't sure why I had returned. Then we kissed again, for a longer time.

"You've never kissed a woman before, have you?"

I shook my head.

"I'm coming back. I'll stay for the weekend. I want to get to know you."

I held my breath while I thought of what to say. "Yes. Okay. Come back," I said.

She kissed me again and said, "Okay. I'm going, but stay. Stay in the room. Hang out here. Do whatever you want. Enjoy it." She handed me a key on a big clunky key chain.

I gave her my home phone number. And I did stay for a few minutes, but I was discombobulated and needed to get my bearings. I just sank into the couch and stared. What had just happened? I grabbed a pastry and took a bite, then threw it back into the box. Seconds later, I raced out and went to my next appointment, feeling utterly and completely turned on and excited for the next day, but frantic that what I had just done was wrong—girls don't kiss girls. It wasn't right. Everything was spinning in my head. One thing was clear: I couldn't wait for her to come back. At my apartment I called Iris to ask her who Sandra Bernhard was.

"She's a huge American comedian. She's friends with Madonna. She's very big right now. Controversial, but funny."

That next morning Sandra called me at home.

"Patricia, I'm on my way back to Paris, but I had to tell you that you're on the front page of the *Herald Tribune*! From the show yesterday. One big photo and it is of you."

"You're kidding!"

"That means we're meant to be, you know that, right? I stepped off a plane and there you were," she said.

My world was about to be completely different, but one that would remain secret to most everyone in my life. What Sandra had said, about us being meant to be, made sense. She and I were meant to be. Knowing that meant the greatest joy in my life would be a dirty secret as well. Being on the front page of the newspaper was enormous. My mother would be so happy. It was weird to share that news with her but not be able to share the news about the woman I just met. My life with Sandra would remain a soul-sucking lie. Just thinking of my feelings for her made me feel like a fraud. Still, the pull was so great, so overwhelming, I knew, holding the phone to my ear, I'd stepped into a life I could not turn my back on.

Chapter Twenty-One

After Comme des Garçons, the floodgates opened for me. Three months after first meeting Karl, I received another break from him. My agent called to tell me.

"Patricia," she said. "I have some really good news," she started to tell me in English.

"Stop, stop. Speak in French. I can understand French better," I said. By that time it was true. My French wasn't as good as my Spanish, obviously, but it beat my English.

"Karl wants to shoot you again, but this time for a campaign. You're going to be the face of Lagerfeld in Asia."

She didn't have to explain to me why this was a huge opportunity. He was the most powerful man in the industry. This meant one big thing: real money. Finally. Campaigns paid money.

"Your face, Patricia," she said. "In Asia."

The studio we shot in this time was super white, not dark like his first one. The other difference was that I'd gained an enormous amount of confidence since that shoot. I felt good. Secure. Like last time, he was dressed in black, but instead of seven assistants there were only three. Also, while he'd had a strong, commanding personality the first time I met him, this time he seemed to be even more in control, as if maybe he'd grown more confident too, which was odd considering who he was and how important he was in the industry. The same hair and makeup team worked on me, and he dressed me in super-chic clothes. Clean, modern, breathtaking. But, like last time, when it was over I felt just a little bit gutted. Working had become fantasy—an escape. When it was finished, I had to own up to my reality.

Next, Karl let me walk in his show, giving me four different looks to wear—or, as we called them in the business, four exits. A few more shows followed. Karl loved hanging out with Sandra, so when she was in town he would have us over for dinner. He was so gracious; once he invited my mother and me to dinner at one of his seven houses in Paris on Rue de l'Université. Even at his home, in a casual setting, he was still the legend. He was smart, a true intellectual, sophisticated, and a generous host. At first I just felt honored he took a liking to me and brought me into his circle. I was nothing like him. Moreover, he was an inspiration to me. He was creative without boundaries. He had vision and made things happen. He made me believe anything was possible. My world was always about struggle, where things weren't possible. Karl proved the opposite to be true.

My mother came to see me work too. Occasionally someone would ask about Sandra in front of her. I'd have to say, "She doesn't know," but it was always okay because she didn't speak English. Karl was so kind to my mother. My mother called when she got back to Venezuela to tell me she heard someone buzzing the apartment. They buzzed a couple of times before she could get to answer it. She was floored to discover it was a delivery for her. Karl had sent her a beautiful box containing an expensive set of pearls.

She was so happy about my success, and she knew who Karl was, so for her to have shared that experience with me—having dinner at Karl Lagerfeld's home—she felt such pride. When she called to tell me he had pearls delivered, I could hear the joy in her voice—not because he'd sent her the pearls, but because everything began to feel positive and significant, as if things were finally going our way. Since those weren't words we'd exchange—we weren't emotional—we spent the call laughing about the pearls. They were so precious and gorgeous.

I said, "Mamá, whatever you do, don't wear them. You'll get killed on the street with them, they're so nice."

In that moment, after she'd had a glimpse into my life, I knew we were both happy. We shared a good laugh about the pearls needing to be locked up. But behind the smile there existed a real sadness. Sharing my love for

Sandra with my mother would have cured it. Sharing my happiness with her would have been liberating. Instead, the lie remained intact. It wasn't so much about coming clean with everything happening; I just wanted to share. I craved her support and approval. More important, though, was her happiness, so I held back despite the pull to hear what she had to say about everything going on, not just the professional side of my life. My professional successes compensated for my being gay, because being gay meant I wasn't good enough. It made me feel like I had to work harder. It meant, too, that I was a weirdo. I judged myself harshly, never mind anyone else judging me. In modeling and fashion we were accepting of the gay guys, of course, but I had always felt bad for them. As I laughed with my mother, my joy was diluted by the realization that I was now one of those people I felt sorry for.

Chapter Twenty-Two

After so many shoots and experiences, the difference between good or great photographers and terrible ones became glaringly evident. The terrible ones would say, "Give me a smile." The worst ones would say, "Give it to me." They didn't understand the vibe you needed to develop with a model. Much later in my career, if a photographer spoke to me like that, my response would be, "No. Not doing this." They'd ask, "Why not?" I'd say nothing. When a photographer talked like that, it was disgusting. No one can tell a model to give it to them or smile—that's condescending, like I am less than or serving them. As I gained popularity and the shoots became grander, I started to encounter the same big-name photographers again and again—some of the amazing ones: Patrick Demarchelier, Sante D'Orazio, Herb Ritts, Paolo Roversi, Francesco Scavullo, and Albert Watson. Working with each of them was like a dance. It was art, and when you looked at photos afterward by these talented photographers, you could always tell that genius went into them. I looked at myself in the photos, and the experience revealed itself to be a piece of art. You could see it in a photo.

A few months after meeting Sandra, I was on a Frida Kahlo–themed shoot with a great photographer in Puerto Vallarta. We often got sent to some very off the beaten path places; the tourist boards wanted to promote them, so they'd work with magazines to get people there. Africa was a hot spot for exotic shoots, and eventually Mexico became one as well. This place was traditionally Mexican-looking: rustic and quaint, small, but very expensive—a place only wealthy people visited. It was a five-star resort right on the water. I was in love with Sandra by this point, and while we lived apart—she in Los Angeles and me in Paris—our relationship had progressed quickly. I'd found a sense of belonging with her—that feeling. That connection. When I wasn't with her, I felt like something was missing. All of a sudden, with Sandra in my life, everything kind of made sense. Thoughts of her surfaced while in such a romantic and pretty place—I wanted to share it with her. The photographer on the shoot was named Pierre; I had worked with him a few times. As we worked, he would say things, like, "Are you okay?" or "I love what you're doing."

We were shooting in this beautiful location on the ocean, and he and I had almost immediately caught our stride. He let me find my moments that day during the shoot, whatever they were, and then he captured them perfectly. He was anticipating my intentions as I moved, in sync with my energy and I with his. He clicked at the right moments; I moved and he clicked. He didn't even have to say anything; we just had this great day shooting together, getting caught up in our work. He was incredible most days, but on that one in particular, we truly hit it off and made beautiful photos together.

At the end of the day, we had dinner at the hotel with the crew, as usual. There were maybe eight of us at a big table. I remember eating delicious corn soup. Pierre sat next to me at dinner. Even when we weren't working, he had a certain sweetness to him, a softness almost, as he spoke and in his gestures. He wasn't overtly flirting, but his eye contact and occasional touches gave me the impression he was attracted to me. We all had some wine with dinner, and since it was our last night and we were leaving the next day, we were all having fun.

Pierre leaned over and whispered to me, "Shall we take a walk after dinner?"

Two thoughts raced through my head before answering: I'm madly in love with Sandra and I'm not gay. "Sure," I said. I wanted to prove to myself I still liked men. We sort of stayed back at the table as everyone drifted off, and then we went for a stroll along a narrow cobblestone street. He was talking about work and some projects, but I wasn't paying attention. I was thinking about Sandra—how easy she had made it for me, how loving she'd been, how we had learned to communicate despite the language barrier between us. They say if you want to learn a language when you're in a foreign country, date someone living there. We figured it out, she and I, despite having no common language. It was challenging because we had no cell phones then. It hit me hard as Pierre and I walked that I was dating a girl, a famous one at that. I'd only told one person: Iris. But I was too ashamed to tell anyone else, not that there were really any friends to tell with my constant travel—on and off planes with a day's notice for shoots in faraway places. Also, I was too ashamed to admit it to even myself.

So when Pierre said, "Would you like to come up to my room? I'll show you the photos," I said yes. Not that I'd paid attention to which photos we'd talked about. I didn't care that he was married or that I was attached. Going to his room probably meant that we would have sex, and I was okay with it. I stared at the pretty red lights that twinkled on the street, strung up in the darkness, as we made our way back to the hotel.

Am I gay or not? That's what I debated as we walked down the hallway to his room. *I'm not. I'm not gay.* I was prepared to prove it, even though being disloyal to Sandra was troubling. If I was gay, that meant I was never going to be with any man again. That meant no marriage, no children. That was too much for me to accept.

Pierre unlocked his door, and we went in and sat on his bed. It was a tiny room, tinier than mine. The walls were stucco, with those little points like whipped cream, and the bedding was simple and white. He was so tidy, tidier than most men. That was an attractive trait. But he had a feminine demeanor to him, so it wasn't a surprise.

We sat close together. He showed me some photos he'd taken weeks before. They were beautiful. His sweetness came through on the paper. The shoot was from Paris. I looked at Pierre, and his faint moustache and dark hair with deep-looking eyes, which told his story when he spoke of each picture, and thought of all the times I had gone home and my aunts repeatedly asked, "When are you going to get married, Patricia?" And my mom always unknowingly protecting my lie, jumping in saying, "Leave her alone."

I'm not gay. I said it over in my head as I sat there on his bed. Then I gently kicked off my sandals.

He leaned in and kissed me on the cheek. Softly. Then I looked at him and we kissed on the lips.

I'm going to hurt you, Sandra, but I'm not a cheater. I need to prove I'm not gay. That's what went through my head.

If she ever found out, it would be horrible—awful—but there was no stopping. It had to be done. Pierre and I had broken the ice, so to speak, on our shoots together, so our bodies fell comfortably into each other. He wore all white and I wore a little sundress, and we peeled off each other's clothing. When you worked with someone like Pierre, a certain level of intimacy developed. He shot close to my skin. He'd seen me in bathing suits. We didn't have to work past that discomfort or shyness; we were long past that already. So we kissed fast, and tenderly, but I didn't want to waste time. I wanted to get it done to prove I was still straight. When we finished having sex, he asked me to stay and spend the night. I said no, that I was going to my room. In my head I thought, *I just needed to prove one thing, and I did.* There was no middle ground for me—a person was gay or not gay. Being gay was not for me.

Back in my room I showered, scrubbing myself with force everywhere, even putting my fingers inside of me to scrub myself clean of him. And then nothing. I went to sleep. I felt really guilty about hurting Sandra but knew deeply in my heart that she was so wonderful that, if she knew why and what I was going through, she would understand. She was so much more elevated than I was spiritually. I had such a love for her in that moment, lying in my own bed that night.

This photo of me was taken when I was 5 and
we were living in Mexico.

Me dancing in a recital in my hometown.

My sister Limaryi and I in New York just after
she and her husband moved there.

My handsome friend Gonzalo and I at a party in New York in 1995 with Jeanne Beker in the background.

The always smiling Lisa in London in the late '90s.

I took my mother, Lidela (or Lila as the grandkids call her) to Rome in 2000 to see Pope John Paul II.

I brought Evelyn, my mom Lidela, and Gaby (left to right) with me to walk the red carpet for *The Mummy Returns* premiere in Los Angeles in 2001.

Iris and I at the Ford offices in Paris
taken with a Polaroid camera.

Lisa took this picture of me back stage before I walked in the
Jean Paul Gaultier show. The spirit of his work that night inspired
me to build up the courage to reveal my truth to my mother.

Fernando, Juan, me, Caty, Carlos, and Limayri
in East Hampton in 2012.

Mario, Juan, Dad and Caty
at a party in Maracaibo.

Maya when she was two.

Part Three

Chapter Twenty-Three

Sitting still in one place was never a great strength of mine.

The upside of success, especially in the wake of the *Marie Claire Bis* cover, was constant travel to exotic places. The downside of success was constant travel to exotic places. I would often head to the airport not even certain exactly where I was headed each day, checking my ticket en route. My life was another country, another plane, another shoot, another missed wedding, family function, or chance to connect with a friend. It did, however, give me the opportunity to fly my mother out to join me on occasion, usually somewhere nice. I had a shoot in Curaçao once, and since it was a short trip, she joined me there. The hotel we were staying in had previously been a hospital. It seemed some bad things had once happened to people within those walls; it gave me a strange feeling when I arrived. It was a beautiful place to stay but a little creepy.

The shoot was for a German clothing company. I had been the face of their catalogue, and for this shoot they were going to take pictures of me out on a yacht. That company had become a good source of income for me. I thought it would be fun for my mom out at sea on the boat. I'd never been on a boat ride like this with my mother—we'd never taken a cruise or anything like that. We had been on small boats for extremely short trips on Margarita Island.

I got my hair and makeup done, and we boarded the boat. There was quite a crowd there; as you can imagine, it takes a lot of people for any shoot. It was a long ride to this little tiny island where we'd do the shoot.

We were two hours off land, and we were still not at our location. It was remote. I didn't see anything other than water all around. I was wearing something white, up against this striking crystal blue tropical water. It was beautiful, but the water became very choppy.

Out of nowhere, while we were still driving, my mom started struggling to breathe with a look of panic on her face. Not wanting to draw attention, she seemed to have waited a little while before telling me, but then finally she did.

"Patricia, my body is too tight," she said. "I can't move."

I took one last look at her, stood up, and yelled, "Is there a doctor on board?"

The producer said, "No, but we are very close to a little island. Maybe they have one."

I had to think quickly. Would the island have enough care if she was truly ill? I felt the burden of a life-altering decision. "No, we have to go back. What if the island doesn't have a hospital?"

Nobody moved. They all looked at each other.

"We've gotta go back now," I kept saying over and over. That meant the shoot wasn't going to happen.

I thought she was having a heart attack because she was basically paralyzed, holding her chest, lying down on the floor of the boat. It was excruciating and horrible to watch, not knowing if she was going to make it or not, or if we'd get back in time for her to get help. I put ice on her neck and kept saying, "Stay calm, hold on, don't worry." I had to be calm, and I actually always am in these situations of chaos. I wasn't calm on the inside, but I was working hard, trying to shift the focus from me to the person who was in front of me, my mother.

The boat turned around. They just floored it, and even though it had taken us two hours to get out there, it was just one hour to get back. Still, it was the longest hour of my life. I kept trying to put my mother's legs up, but they were stiff. We couldn't move her. Of course, she was more worried about me and kept asking if the clients were okay or upset.

Here's what was really crazy: we made it back, and the minute she stepped off the boat and put her feet on land, she was fine. As if nothing had happened. She felt horrible for me, and she didn't even want to go to the hospital. I insisted we go, however, to have her checked out, and the doctors said she'd had a panic attack and hyperventilated.

My mom and I never spoke about that day again, not for any particular reason except it didn't seem important. It was one of those things that happen and then it's done. From what they told me at the hospital, I thought my mom had become sick from the waves because the boat was moving a lot when we got out there. So it felt like it was a closed subject.

I never told her that the client never called me again either. Once people see any sort of crack or fragility, they don't want to be around you anymore. But there's something else about fragility, something I didn't realize at the time. In my life I'd never witnessed any weakness in my mom. My stoic mother, the strongest woman I have ever known, had some fragility buried deep inside her indigenous soul. I didn't understand until many years later that my lie had contributed to keeping it buried.

My life revolved around work. Otherwise, whenever possible, I'd try to meet Sandra in LA or sometimes where she was working, or she'd come to meet me. I was receiving a taste of American culture from an amazing vantage point. We hung around a lot of famous people because that was her life. We attended a benefit once on a trip to LA. It was in a giant room with white cotton–covered tables filling the space. The weather was gorgeous, and the mood in the room vibrant and happy. I was seated next to a beautiful buxom blonde woman with this crazy twang of an accent. She resembled the people I'd seen on TV on shows like *Dallas*. She had a cowboy look to her and was incredibly nice. The benefit, the woman—it all felt so American to me, or what I'd always imagined America to be.

In the car afterward I asked Sandra about the larger-than-life character I'd chatted with during the meal.

It was Dolly Parton.

I was deeply in love with Sandra in a way I'd never experienced before. We'd built a trust so strong, I felt I could put my life in her hands and she would handle it with care. When I hurt, she hurt. When she hurt, I hurt. It was an unimaginable connection. We protected each other, loved each other, and had become two parts of one whole.

As a side bonus, my English was improving dramatically. Communicating with Sandra had forced me to learn it. Despite my happiness and professional success, there was a thin layer of angst that enveloped me. One rare weekend when I was actually in Paris and not on the road, both Katie and I were at Iris's apartment. No one in my family knew about Sandra still, but Katie and Iris did. It was somewhat of a relief for me to at least let it all hang out there with them. Both were the most wonderfully open-minded people one could ever have the good fortune of being friends with. Sharing with them was easy, comfortable, and safe. There was no judgment toward me. The modeling world in general held that same mind-set. It was an open place full of gay people and straight people alike, and no one cared what anyone else was doing between the sheets.

"Are you happy?" Iris asked one night in her apartment.

"Yeah," I said. "Very happy. But this is so hard. She's in LA. I'm here. It's exhausting, but more than that I want to be close to her. I miss her when I'm not with her." I didn't dare say that it ate away at me to pretend to be straight with most everyone in my family. It didn't seem right to mention my efforts to protect them from the shameful truth of my sexuality, which I still hadn't fully accepted to be true. Sandra, I loved. Being gay, not so much.

Katie was walking around the apartment doing some work, getting some things organized. Hearing our conversation, she stopped, looked at me, and said, "Would you like to go to New York? I think it's time."

My answer was easy. New York was on the agenda, and had it not been for Sandra, maybe that move would have occurred months or a year later, but given the situation, it seemed appropriate and right. I nodded yes, grateful for her gesture.

"I think you're ready. We're ready for you there," Katie said.

At first when I moved to New York, I stayed with one of Sandra's friends in her apartment on the Upper West Side at 97th Street. It was generous of a stranger, essentially, to let me in, but she had seven cats and I was allergic. They kept peeing on my belongings. When Sandra came to town, she'd always stay at the Royalton Hotel, so I'd join her there. I was grateful to Sandra for awakening me to the love she had to offer, and for our life and time together. I learned so much from her, not just about relationships but also about really basic matters that were completely foreign to me. I observed, asked a ton of questions, and therefore gained an understanding during our early days together in the States about items such as frequent-flier miles, and how to use credit cards—all the mundane tasks that were not part of my world. I picked up a lot from her friends too.

Soon after my arrival in the city, Sandra came to visit. We went downtown for dinner at the apartment of her best friend—a young designer named Isaac. He lived somewhere around 12th Street in a fabulous apartment.

Obviously, Sandra had told him that I was a model who had been working in Paris. As we sipped pre-dinner cocktails in his living room, he explained he was a designer. I was unfamiliar with his work and assumed he was trying to break into design.

"Darling, would you do me the honor of being in my show?" he asked. He was energetic with wavy-curly hair.

I thought to myself, *I guess I can do this guy a favor. He's getting started and he needs an experienced model to walk in his show.*

"Sure," I said.

Later, when I realized it was Isaac Mizrahi and what a big deal he was, I understood he was doing me—or more likely Sandra—the favor.

"Patricia just moved here," Sandra said. "She doesn't know where to live. She needs a place."

"Well, darling," he said, "if you're going to live here, you absolutely need to live on 12th Street or below on the West Side. Don't let anyone tell you otherwise."

I listened, having no idea who this guy was, unaware it was the start of his ascent into the upper echelon of the fashion world. He seemed to know about real estate, so for the next three days I looked at places in the West Village with a real estate agent until settling on 299 West 12th Street, apartment 6E. It was a beautiful one-bedroom that Sandra helped me decorate.

Many things about working in New York revealed themselves to me quickly. Being an experienced model coming over from France had caché, but the Americans had worked more with the Italians. No one in the United States knew me. Plus, New York was an entirely different ball game. There was a pecking order and a different way of doing shows.

That first season I only got hired for two shows, including Isaac's. The other big show was from Carolina Herrera. She was Venezuelan, and she gave me a chance. In Paris I might have walked in thirty to forty shows in that same season. In New York I had to work to land what came my way. There was work, but it wasn't pouring in as it had in Paris. Part of it had to do with my look. I looked like everyone walking the streets of New York. Ordinary. In Europe that look was exotic. The streets of New York were filled with Latinas like me from Puerto Rico, Mexico, the Dominican Republic, and other Hispanic places. Not so in France, where that look was considered special.

New York was different in other ways as well. There was a bonus to the city: the workdays were very well structured and organized. A shoot that would last from 6:00 a.m. to 2:00 a.m. in France would be 9:00 a.m. to 5:00 p.m. in the United States. But, in a sense, I was coming down a few levels, starting from scratch to re-establish myself in the new landscape, in a new marketplace with new people. That's not to say there wasn't money coming in, good money.

Still, there were rough moments that led me to question my move. Bouts of longing for Paris washed over me some days, despite the happiness I felt being that much closer to Sandra. There were days when the fine line between elation and depression were blurred. Sandra was famous, so the paparazzi followed her, and word of her having a girlfriend had spread since I'd arrived in the States. Sandra was in *Out* magazine talking openly about her sexuality, but she never outed me publicly. The press generally seemed to leave me alone, but occasionally my photo walking with her would get caught in the crossfire when we'd run to a taxi or see them coming and bolt. Once there was a very close call. A Venezuelan newspaper picked up Sandra's story in *Out*, identifying me as her girlfriend. I panicked and made a quick call home to tell my dad it wasn't true. I was most worried he'd be the one reading it and be the most upset. But he believed me.

The concern about my secret life being revealed was mounting and the pressure to hide it increasing. Keeping my eye on that news traveling to my home country was a lot of work, but luck had been on my side mostly. The stress was real, and the sadness of the secret never fully left me, but it was occasionally diluted by the work and the enjoyment it provided.

Chapter Twenty-Four

Sandra traveled with me once to Venezuela, introduced only as a very famous friend of mine who lived in LA. The fact that we lived in two different cities helped alleviate suspicion. It also wasn't even something my family considered about me, that there'd be a girl in my life in that way, so the anxiety was somewhat self-generated. To them, it was an unimaginable lifestyle. For me, I'd live openly in the United States, and then I would return home and tuck it all in. It didn't feel good, but it felt manageable and necessary.

Early on, when visiting home, Jorge would call to say hello. He'd started a modeling agency that groomed other girls for the pageant. On the trip there with Sandra, while she was still at my house writing, I went to visit Jorge's office for the first time. He was eager for me to see his new accomplishment. The space was small, but my picture was everywhere. He had discovered me, and he was proud of that success. He thrived on what we'd accomplished together.

He didn't look good when he walked into the waiting room to greet me. He looked frail. He kissed both my cheeks and took me back to his office, where he spoke with great animation about what he'd set up there. There was, however, a slight strain to our conversation, but I wasn't sure why.

"This is where we teach the girls to walk, Patricia," he said. There was a mini stage set up.

"I'm happy to come speak to the girls sometime if you need me to," I said.

"That would be great. I'd love you to be involved if you have time."

"Are you taking care of yourself, Jorge?" I asked him.

He sat down in a chair. Gestured for me to do the same. He looked at the ground when he spoke.

"I'm HIV positive, Patricia," he said. "I just found out."

Rage came over me initially. It should have been compassion. I'd seen men deteriorate from this disease and be mistreated for having it. It was awful. I lived through the era when all this had started to emerge, and I should have felt more for Jorge in that moment. My anger toward him was anger toward the world and everyone I'd seen die from this terrible disease.

"Jorge, in this day and age? How could you be so reckless?" My judgment was unfair.

There was nothing he could say. He knew he was being judged.

We talked a little more. I made it clear that my friendship and gratitude toward him were endless, but I left confused by what else I could do and furious he'd gotten HIV. He'd blown all his hard work and contracted a disease that could have been avoided. I owed him probably more warmth and love than I gave him that day. I continued to keep in touch on the phone when he called, but not with much enthusiasm on my part. I knew he was spiraling downward. I just didn't know how rapidly then.

The first Christmas I went home without Sandra was agony. The music was always playing in my mother's place, and the mood was always celebratory. Sandra would call on our home line. It made me sad that she was missing all the fun and food and happiness in my home. My two realities were completely at odds with each other. It was awful. I would always speak to her in English. I knew my mother couldn't understand what I was saying, but still I felt anxiety—just like when I was a teenager on the phone with a boy. There was always panic that my mother would pick up the phone in another room and hear something that would completely shock her. It was overwhelming for me to juggle all the worries that came home with me.

My mother would always cook chicken soup. Just the smell of her food gave me a feeling of warmth and comfort, especially when I'd first walk in the door, making me question, *Why can't I tell her about my life? Why can I not tell my mother I'm gay?* I'd eat the soup and the Venezuelan bread called *arepa*, and with every bite the notion that I was dishonest and a liar deepened. At the same time, it felt like maybe it would be okay to say something and reveal myself. Then I'd worry that all the success I'd achieved would be replaced by absolute disappointment. That my mom had finally gotten a nice place to live and didn't have to struggle wouldn't matter if her daughter were in love with a woman.

So instead of saying anything, when the stress really started to strangle me in my mother's kitchen or as we all sat smiling and laughing around the Christmas tree, I'd get my Discman, turn up the music, step outside, and run up and down the stairs in the hallway, lost in my thoughts, alone in my reality. When I had an urge to share my secret, I'd quickly tell my family I needed to work out and work off all the Christmas eating—up and down, up and down again until it was out of my system. I was so deep into my thoughts that I didn't notice until I stopped that my legs were killing me.

I'm such a weirdo, I'd say over and over in my head, as I pushed my heart rate higher for the workout. Sometimes on those stairs I'd even question my relationship with Sandra. Looking at my life in the United States while I was in Venezuela made me consider that I was lost with her too—alone in a foreign country where I didn't belong. My family assumed the stairs were part of my quest to stay thin for my job, but it was simply my escape—my place to think about my dual life and Sandra and my secret. I felt desperate, like a complete outsider in my home among the people I was closest to. I didn't belong anywhere. After an hour on the stairs, I'd shake it all off, rejoin the festivities, and become a daughter and sister. The door to my mother's home was like a trans-formation tunnel: walking through it meant shedding the real me and becoming the perfect, successful, loving, and straight daughter.

When I wasn't on stairs, I was on planes. I'd smoke and drink coffee and alcohol, trying not to feel anything. Life was blurry, almost on pur-pose. My life was just about me going and going, running from my truth whenever I could.

Chapter Twenty-Five

More than a year into my time in the United States, my life was taking off professionally. My second season in New York, I walked in almost every show—thirty of them. I was in my apartment in New York one night when the phone rang. It was my sister Limayri with a shocking announcement.

She had traveled to the Dominican Republic, met a guy, and eventually married him. Of course, I had missed the wedding because I was working, but I missed everything in those days. That wasn't the news.

"Guess what?" she said.

"We're moving to New York, Phil and I!" She was excited.

My chest tightened. I couldn't breathe. My worlds were colliding, and there was nothing I could do to prevent it from happening.

I managed to say, "That's great," but my mind was racing. What was I going to do? Phil had grown up in New York and wanted to move back. I didn't know him well. I had sort of not kept up on anything at home. I was too busy modeling to really have paid attention to the possibility of them ending up in my city.

"When are you guys coming?" I asked, dropping myself onto a couch in my living room.

"Soon. I'm pregnant! So within the month we'll be there! We want to have the baby in New York."

Lost in my thoughts, I was barely able to congratulate her or give her the enthusiasm she deserved.

This was much more serious than Fernando arriving in Spain to find me living with a boyfriend. I was going to have to tell my sister I was gay. The days that followed that call, I felt consumed with panic. Everywhere I walked, every subway ride, I looked for a sign to help me deal with the situation. Sleep eluded me. Distraught, I stared out the window late at night, kicking myself for thinking this day would never come. Of course my worlds would eventually meet. I was naive to have thought otherwise. In the midst of all my stress leading up to her arrival, there was one inkling inside me that was positive: the thought that a family member would be there with me for the first time since Fernando. This one tiny thread of positivity helped me keep it together those weeks while I waited. I allowed myself to grow excited about the possibility of my sister being in New York all the time. I'd always marveled when people went to spend a Friday night with their families while I'd eat at home alone.

The sign finally arrived. Sometimes the smallest gestures in life have the largest, most profound impact.

Compared to many, my life was amazing—there was no denying that. Even at my lowest points, gratitude always rang clear in my mind. My life had love, professional success, and an amazing family. I had my health and I had money coming in. But the strain of my secret weighed heavily on me, and grappling with coming clean and sticking out as a model in New York had started to wear me down. There also seemed to be a negative attitude toward Hispanics, which was most pronounced when I'd get back to the United States after a trip home. It wasn't as significant in New York, but there was a second-class citizen feeling when I'd return from a trip. No one of Latin descent had really made a mark in Hollywood, on the runway, or in a business that was visible to the masses. I wasn't exactly treated with any direct prejudice, but the magazine covers didn't approach me, which seemed to be due to my being Latina. The industry in the US was very well defined: beautiful, blonde, all-American-looking girls. That was beauty. Period.

One weekend afternoon, walking around 14th Street, a girl on the street approached me. Before she even spoke she wrapped her arms around me, hugging and crying. It scared me at first. It was random, unexpected. She looked like she knew me. Then she spoke.

"Patricia!" she said. She was young, maybe twenty years old, with dark features, clearly Latina.

"Yes," I said, stopping.

"I just wanted to say thank you," she said.

"For what?" I asked, somewhat confused.

"Thank you for making us Latinas feel worthy. You have no idea how much that means to me. To my friends. You make us feel proud of who we are. I used to feel bad about myself, but now when I see you in a magazine . . . well, you changed that. You make me feel beautiful to be Latin."

I felt visible suddenly. I felt like myself, not the girlfriend of someone else, or the daughter, or the sister. I was *me*. My own person. God was telling me not to be upset or give up. That I was doing what I was doing for a reason, redefining beauty for my people and making a mark in a place that hadn't been marked. Moved doesn't begin to describe my feelings that day. Pride overwhelmed me. Happiness pulsed through me. Being given the opportunity to do something that made someone else feel good was the greatest gift and reward imaginable. The money suddenly didn't matter. The number of shows and the big magazines would come, but in that moment I didn't care. It was an instant shift in my mood and attitude that occurred within seconds of that encounter. The work—it was all going to come my way. It was going to happen. A breakthrough for the Latina community was pending. That girl and people like her were the reason. Her kind words verified that it was all going to take place. People who looked like me were going to feel good and be recognized for their beauty and strength. I thanked that girl that day. I owed her more appreciation than I could have shown her in a few short minutes. Her words didn't wash away the feelings left by the lie I lived, but at least they gave me strength to understand that good was coming of my life despite my secret, not just bad feelings and anxiety about everything. I was desperate to protect my family and my mother, mostly from the disappointment they would feel if they knew whom I loved and how I loved, but this brief encounter gave me answers about what I was doing and why I was doing it all.

When my sister and Phil finally got to town, they rented an apartment up on 48th Street and 2nd Avenue. I vividly remember taking a taxi up there immediately after they arrived. I was terrified to tell her, not only because of what she'd think but also because she was pregnant and the shock didn't seem healthy. But getting busted and having her hear it another way wasn't an option. The only real choice was to tell her—straight out. There was no other alternative. Selfishly, too, I needed to be able to share the information with someone I loved. I'd left my country years before, and while her reaction was an unknown variable, having one family member at my side would help ease my anxiety.

They had a tiny one-bedroom apartment. I went up in the elevator, knocked on her door, and met her husband for the first time. He was on his way out to run an errand, so after he greeted me he left. My sister was showing—looking glowing and gorgeous at seven months despite being exhausted from the move. I felt bad making our meeting about me. They had one small rectangular Ikea table and two chairs. I sat on the table, not on a chair, and wasted no time. She was in the kitchen, but I was too nervous to sit with it any longer, so I just blurted out, "I have something to tell you. I have a girlfriend. I've been hanging out with Sandra. A lot." The word gay didn't come out of my mouth. That wasn't easy to say or even to admit to myself. "I mean . . . I'm always hanging out with Sandra."

Limayri had been getting me a glass of water. She came out from the galley kitchen and said, "Oh, I know." She was totally nonchalant about it.

"What do you mean, you know?"

"Well," she said, "you are always with her, you travel with her, you brought her home: What do you think? I'm stupid?"

"Why didn't you ever tell me you knew?"

"If you don't tell me," she said, "why am I going to tell you?"

I was still worried. "Do you care?"

"If you're happy, I'm happy. And you know what? Caty knows too."

"My little sister, Caty?" I asked.

"Yeah. We've talked about it a lot."

My shoulders dropped and I let out a breath. I felt a huge sense of relief. An immediate feeling of love washed over me for my sisters as well. As if she was reading my mind as it spun forward, she said, "But don't tell Mamá." We both laughed.

The situation with Limayri had not played out the way I'd anticipated. Fear had blurred it for me and made it seem like there would be only dire consequences, which couldn't have been more wrong. Everything came out completely different from what I had expected—so much better. I had trained my thoughts and my heart to expect the absolute worst. That's the way I approached most everything. It was a lesson learned.

Obviously, this news wouldn't play out so great at home with my parents. Catholicism and religion were too huge in my country for me to tell them. If I'd grown up somewhere else in the Western world, maybe it would have been easier. Maybe it would have been acceptable or easy to talk about, but that wasn't the case. I struggled with it. Everyone gay had to struggle around that time, not just in Venezuela. I watched Sandra and the guys in fashion who were out struggle. They all led challenged lives. Somehow, not saying it maybe helped me avoid the struggles or at least pretend I could. Sandra experienced pain and discrimination even though she was hugely successful. She had problems that probably stemmed from being gay. Every gay person did. Not that most straight people didn't have problems—we all did. But being gay brought on a different stack of crises. There was a common sadness among gay people, and that had been my only experience with them, despite achieving tremendous levels of success. Hiding it made me not weird, not as sad. On the outside anyway.

Telling my sister, however, was a gift.

Sandra and I didn't last much longer beyond that point. We were growing in different ways. She was thirty-nine at the time and wanted to have a baby. I wasn't ready for that, and I was just coming into my own. I was young—in my early twenties—and terrified of the commitment of a child. Plus, with my career and my sisters knowing my secret, I felt reborn almost and started to see a different life ahead of me. Inevitably we broke up. I checked into the Mondrian Hotel in LA and for some reason felt compelled to stay there crying my eyes out for a full week. I wasn't sure exactly why, but I did. In some small way, I wanted to stay to punish myself. I felt I owed her that much. And I wanted to remain close to her for just a little longer.

Chapter Twenty-Six

New York eventually paid off. I was walking in all the shows there, and I was flying to Paris, London, and Milan to walk in those shows too. New York was a gift, the reward for the endless hours and hard work. In the early days of my career, I got to my shoots via the bus or on foot. I took the train to the airport and around each country I was traveling in Europe. As the shoots and shows grew more significant and frequent, I traveled in black cars with drivers to and from the airport instead of by public transportation. From New York, I once took the Concorde to Paris and back in one day to renew my work visa. My modeling career hadn't quite exploded, but I was making inroads into the inner circle and my lifestyle had shifted. I wasn't quite the main exotic go-to, but I was becoming more mainstay in what was then termed the Glamazon era. Some of the press started referring to me as the first Latina supermodel.

Still, it was unexpected when in the mid-'90s I received a call from Iris in Paris with a sizable opportunity. A company called Gaumont, the Disney of Paris, was about to produce the biggest film ever made to date in France, and they were looking for a female lead. It was called *Le Jaguar*, and it was about saving an Indian village. Filming would take place in the Amazon.

"You should at least meet with the director," she urged. Iris had always been my biggest champion—first in modeling, then suggesting I start acting.

"Iris, I respect actors too much to think I could do this. I'm trained for dance, but not this."

"Will you please just meet with the guy? You're in LA anyway."

Meeting him meant driving myself, which stressed me out. Once I started spending more time in LA, I learned (an overstatement at the time) to drive. I was back and forth between LA and New York frequently, so it made sense. I learned in a Chrysler Sebring. I bought the same car in white I'd learned in—it seemed the smartest thing to do, considering my nervousness on the road. It was funny: some Mexican guy I paid had given me all the answers to the driving test ahead of time, so while I passed it, I had no clue how to drive. Cheating was a great regret every single time I got behind the wheel, because I didn't know what I was doing, as there had been zero studying ahead of the written test. When I finally and inevitably got a ticket, I had to go to traffic school, which thrilled me to no end. It gave me a chance to learn more about the road, and I loved every second of it.

So for my meeting with the director, Francis Veber, we met at a hotel. I gripped the steering wheel with force as I drove, adding to the stress. But it dissipated quickly upon arrival because he was so pleasant. He was a classy guy, and we spoke to each other in French. It was a brief conversation, briefer than expected, but by the time I had driven myself home, I'd learned he'd offered me the job.

The phone was ringing when I walked in the door. Katie gave me the news.

"You need to do this. It's a good opportunity," she said. "Say yes even if you don't want to do more acting after this."

So I did. My agent, Glena Marshall, connected me with Sheila Gray, an acting coach in New York. She worked with all the famous people there. She prepared me for the movie as best she could in the time allotted. I was green, no question, but she gave me the preparation needed to get started.

Two profound gifts emerged from doing the movie. First, I acquired a taste for acting and fell madly in love with it. Second, the movie was shot in both Brazil and Venezuela, so I was able to work at home for the first time since I'd left and see my country in a new way. When I first arrived home as part of the French team, a little bit of friction surfaced among the local production crew because a Venezuelan was coming into Venezuela with the French. As the lead. That lasted all of two seconds, and eventually we all connected as though we'd been friends for a lifetime, shooting among the indigenous people in places in my country I had never seen before, such as Angel Falls—the highest waterfall in the world. I grew to be great friends with so many people on the crew, including Gabriela Nuñez, the unit production manager, who eventually became my best friend. There had once been an accident on set in the rain. A boat had injured an indigenous actor. We were so isolated and remote that there was no way to get a plane in there quickly. Gaby jumped into action and coordinated a massive effort for all of us to grab lights and reflectors and build a makeshift landing strip. She saved this guy's life with her quick thinking. He lost his foot, but he survived.

I grew to love my country again, and in a different way than I had when I left. I hadn't experienced it in quite the same way before. It had always been about lack for me, about struggle. But the people and the country were suddenly full of possibility, not hardship. It was stunning in a way I'd never seen. The people were warm and loving. My entire life, all I'd known was my small town. But Venezuela had so much more to offer that was beyond my comprehension until I was able to return there for work. Reconnecting with my roots in that way was nothing short of a gift.

Jean Reno, one of the lead actors, helped me understand so much about acting and the craft. The way he taught me to approach it made me become enchanted with acting. It was fun too. Francis hated bugs. At one point, deep in the Amazon, we were always plagued with them. He was so intent on keeping away from them that he had his entire house covered in a mosquito net that enveloped the house completely. It made the house look like a UFO.

I got a different bug: the acting bug. As we wrapped up shooting, I made a vow to study more. I had quit smoking for the shoot and gained some weight, which didn't help with my modeling. In fact, some of the work slowly dried up as a result, making me wonder if I should worry about my health or my career. I committed to studying acting. I went so far as to get an apartment in LA, after all those years of resisting doing so when I was with Sandra, so I could focus on my craft and learn all that I could learn.

Chapter Twenty-Seven

Acting and modeling occupied most of my time. So did crying. I cried for two years over Sandra. The sadness that lingered felt as if it would never disappear. It was the first real breakup I'd experienced, and I was unprepared for the intensity of the pain that ensued.

I was working diligently to study acting, living in New York, but with my second home in LA. I continued modeling. While in London during the show season, I was looking for lunch one day. The food there was weak back then, but there had been one place that served excellent tomato soup. I'd eaten it the day before. To prepare for the shows and get as thin as possible, I mostly ate vegetarian—foods like portobello mushrooms replaced steak. When we would do the show circuit, we would eat the least for the first two cities, to get as thin as possible. We'd become so thin that by the time we landed in London or Paris, we could eat a little bit more. I ate a lot of grilled vegetables with olive oil, making it challenging to find something on the run sometimes. It was raining as I rushed from one fashion designer fitting to another. All I could think was, *Where did I get that soup from?* My craving for it was overwhelming. I'd been crying that morning in the shower in my room at Blakes Hotel over Sandra, so the soup would have both filled me up and given me some comfort.

Oddly, that day there was one appointment on my calendar with a photographer's representative in SoHo. Usually it was just designer meetings for the shows. I was scanning my list of addresses to rush to from the back of a car, thinking how strange it was that this one was slotted for noon that day. With my stomach growling, we pulled up to the address. I jumped out of the car and walked into the building. I waited in the lobby until a British woman, the owner of the agency, came out to greet me. She introduced herself as Lisa. I stared at this woman for a second, taking her all in. She was shorter than I was, sweet, with a massive smile. Her hair was curly, and she had enormous, wide blue eyes. Pretty, a little chubby, and she had huge breasts. She had a funky style—executive looking because it was an office, but funky and original. She wore Joseph pants paired with brown boots—an executive combination with an edge to it. The encounter proved that love at first sight actually existed. It was instant for me.

She was checking me out, it seemed, but I wasn't 100 percent certain of how these situations actually worked. We talked about all the shows that I was walking in, which was most of them that season, and she told me which designers she loved. At some point in our conversation, she asked, "There is an exhibit tonight we're all going to. Would you care to join us?" My answer was yes, of course. I knew I liked her, but even if we weren't hanging out romantically, once again the thought of having a friend was enticing. We chatted and agreed to meet later that night for a drink with some other people.

"Where do I meet you?" I asked, not knowing London.

"Let's meet at Balans at, say, seven thirty?" she answered.

I got directions from her, agreed on the plan, and left within ten minutes. We didn't even talk much business. She asked a few questions and later did land me a lot of work. But that day I left mostly curious. The problem was, I didn't know if she was gay or straight. There was something in the way she looked at me that day that was undeniable and very exciting. The uncertainty added to my excitement.

As I walked downstairs I felt joy I hadn't felt in years. I opened the metal door to leave Lisa's building, looking around for the driver, Peter. I had used same driver many times before. Down in SoHo there were all sorts of tiny streets filled with little lunch and sandwich windows. Since Peter was not there and there were tons of places to eat, I decided to grab some food. And what was sitting there feet from Lisa's office building? A sign that said: Tomato Soup. Not just any tomato soup either. It was the place I'd been craving all day, the place where I'd gotten the soup the day before. It was directly below Lisa's building; there was no question it was a sign. I practically sprang to the door, opened it, and went up to the little bar against the wall. There was a small counter where I placed my order.

I stood smiling while I waited, took the soup to go, and stepped back out. I saw my driver and hopped in.

"I'm going to eat soup, so let me know if you're stopping abruptly or something," I said to Peter.

"Of course," he said from the front.

I took a tiny sip from the spoon. It was extremely hot. After a couple of sips of my soup, I said to him, "I think I've just fallen in love."

He said, "Have you? How great, my dear."

There was a phone in the car, so once I finished my soup, I dialed my London agent, Tori, at Models One.

"I think I've fallen in love with a girl at the photographer's agency," I said with excitement.

"You have? Who?"

"Her name is Lisa. We just hit it off."

"Oh, she just called. She liked you too. Big time."

"Wow, we're meeting at Balans later. With some other people, I think."

"I'll join you guys there," Tori said. I thought it odd that she was inviting herself, but I was glad to have a buffer since I didn't know what I was getting into exactly.

The rest of my afternoon was a blur, as I spent it with tremendous excitement thinking about meeting Lisa.

We did meet and laughed a lot that night. Lisa looked hot in a long black leather jacket and black boots. I arrived late, so they'd all been drinking already and were a bit loose by then. But by the end of the night, all was clear: she had indeed been checking me out. For the first time in a very long time, I felt desired. It also made me feel safe enough to put myself out there. Uncertainty makes people vulnerable and self-conscious. No one likes rejection. It hurt too much. But with Lisa I knew immediately that night where I stood. She was direct and went for it. Her power was attractive to me. Plus, there was suddenly the excitement of something new: a new life, a new love. What emerged was the possibility that I deserved something again, which I hadn't felt in forever.

Later, it was revealed that the meeting between Lisa and me wasn't a chance encounter. We were set up to meet. The inner world knew I was gay, so it wasn't secret, but it was Tori and Karen, the agency owner, who had made the connection. Lisa, Tori, and Karen were all great friends and were training for a marathon together. As they ran by a bus stop shelter with my picture on it for Monsoon perfume, Lisa said, "Now that is who I like. She's beautiful. That's a woman I would like to meet."

"We represent her," said Tori.

"Do you really?" asked Lisa.

"Yes, we do, darling," said Karen.

Lisa made it clear she needed to meet me.

I was the only one not in on the setup, but that didn't matter. I fell in love quickly. I hadn't dated much since Sandra. Concern had set in that I'd never truly find love again. It seemed unattainable. But in that moment when I first met Lisa, that all changed like a light switch, and I felt hope. The crying stopped too, which was the greatest part of all.

Chapter Twenty-Eight

Lisa lived in London and I lived in New York, but I spent a considerable amount of time in London because Tori and Karen were getting me so much work there. I was so enthusiastic about having Lisa in my life that the ocean between us didn't matter. It was the prime of my career, but she kicked everything into high gear with her outlook—making good things even better. She had so much joy in her and was full of life all the time. Her smile entered the room before she did. I'd never been around anyone like that—always up. Always happy. Always sharing and spreading her disposition and positive outlook. She was funny to the core. I loved all of that about her.

There was a lot of talk as we approached the year 2000 that the world was going to come to an end. While she was one of the most optimistic people on the planet, she also bought into that notion, so she had an idea. Before the clock struck midnight on the new millennium, she wanted to come clean about her sexuality. She didn't want to have the world end without her mother knowing she was gay. One day in the middle of the week, out of nowhere, Lisa declared that she was ready to tell her family.

I was impressed by how courageous she was for making the decision. I felt more like a coward than ever. I rationalized that England was more open-minded and it would be easier for her. Her mom was close by in Manchester, so it didn't require a lot of planning for her to take a trip. That weekend she traveled to see her mom to break the news. Lisa got her mom drunk first and then told her she was gay. Just like that. It took a while to get her drunk but only a couple of minutes to get the words out. She called me in New York right away afterward and told me she had done it. Her mom had survived the shocking news but was so drunk she fell down the stairs that night. We laughed about the irony, that she hadn't had a heart attack from shock but could have hurt herself falling down the stairs. She was fine, just a little bruised. And she'd taken the news well.

That left me with a heavy burden. Lisa was understanding that I'd do it; I just needed to find the right time and, of course, the courage. For weeks I searched inside myself to find the strength Lisa had shown. It was on my mind because she'd done it. Being Venezuelan made it a little more difficult. The pressures were different. My family was different. Lisa was incredibly respectful of my decision.

One night in Paris, about a month after Lisa had told her mom, I was backstage waiting to walk in a mega show being put on by designer Jean Paul Gaultier. It was just around the time my movie *The Mummy* had released. Lisa was there with me at the show as I got ready. My hair was big and crazy, and they'd painted me with tons of makeup. It had taken four or maybe even six hours in the makeup chair to get ready. It was to be a wild and elaborate show. Gaultier's work was so out there, yet so authentic. Most people who were extremely successful were also extremely unique in character and in their art. That's what made them special. Gaultier was special. It struck me, maybe for the first time, taking it all in backstage: I was unique and special too, and I needed to honor what I'd been given. As I sat there getting ready to walk, I was feeling this great sense of pride thinking about my journey to this moment, the only Latina in this massive show, excited to be a part of something so amazing. Gaultier was a genius, but he was also doing exactly what he wanted to do. It made me realize that I could be myself too. That was the moment, I decided right there. It all just clicked suddenly. I turned to Lisa before I went out onstage.

"I'm ready."

The lie had gone on long enough and done enough damage to my psyche. I dug deep for the guts to come clean with my family. The strangest and most unexpected place had given me strength.

She nodded. She knew exactly what my words meant.

That was one of my favorite shows. I walked that runway feeling strong and free; I even jumped down and sat on some woman's lap. It was instantly liberating and exhilarating, not to mention how weightless everything suddenly felt. Lisa was laughing when I finished and told me she couldn't stop thinking, "Wow, what's gotten into her?" as she watched me.

Filled with resolve, I made plans immediately after that show. It was time to go to Venezuela to tell my mom that I was gay. I was ready.

The ambulance was waiting when I arrived. Not having a clue how bad it would be, I arranged before leaving for Venezuela to have one standing by. I feared my mother would have a heart attack when she heard my news.

Fernando lived in a really funky part of Porlamar on Margarita Island, which was just off the coast. He had married the most amazing woman, Mary, and they had one child by then. It was close to Christmas, so my mom was there for her. I wanted to talk to her face to face, and I wanted her to be the first person in my family I spoke to upon arrival.

Other than that one press report, which attempted to out me when I was with Sandra, I had successfully hidden my sexuality in Venezuela despite my popularity there. If my mom already knew, she had clearly respected me enough not to push me or ask me. She never said a word.

I went upstairs to the apartment and felt a little at ease when the smell of cooking hit me right away, welcoming me home. My mom made sweet bread, *pan dulce*. It had always been one of her favorite things. She grilled it and put butter and cheese on it. She must have made it for my brother because they loved it too. That smell, it made me feel safe.

Before even taking off my jacket or dropping my things, I told my mother to sit down, that we had to talk. We were in the living room. It was late, so my brother and his wife were already in their bedroom.

We sat down beside each other on the couch. It was dimly lit, the tree in the corner illuminating the room. I could have changed my mind, as I had so many times before. I was so nervous but determined. This time was different from all the times before when I'd only pretended to consider telling the truth. Being afraid wasn't a good enough excuse. There was no way back and no other way to handle the situation.

So after taking a deep breath, I just said, "Mamá, it's true. I am gay." Those were the only words that came out.

There was silence inside the apartment, so for a moment I listened to what was outside, briefly wishing I were out there with it. I heard distant firecrackers, which were common at that time of the year. I waited for my mom to say something, listening to all the popping sounds instead, interrupted once by a car blasting loud, strong salsa music. The music faded in, then out, as the car passed. Then my mother broke the silence in the room as she started to cry. Panic set in. My mom, she didn't express herself very much. She was a proud woman, stoic, so I wasn't sure if she'd say anything, or if I'd ever even know what she was thinking at that moment, or how she felt about my news. Wayuu people don't reveal themselves too much. Indigenous women, they are very quiet and shy. They don't look you in the eye sometimes because they're so shy. So when she finally did look up to speak, after a minute had passed, I knew it was a big thing for her.

"My poor daughter. I can only imagine how hard it must have been for you all these years—all these years trying to tell me something and not being able to do it," she said as she held my hand.

I was overwhelmed by her peace and sense of calm, not to mention how giving and loving she was being at that moment. It was simply amazing. I was so moved by her words.

"I don't understand, it's true. I can't tell you that I ever will," she said. "It's hard for me to understand that world, but I'm here for you and I love you."

Cherished words. It must have been so difficult for her to say them, as a Latina woman, as an indigenous woman. I also vividly remember the happiness I felt when I looked down through the window from the sixth floor and the ambulance, as directed by a quick call on my part, pulled away, reminding me that things would be okay, that the truth was okay. What was funny was that I heard a gunshot when I looked out, as we often did there, and I told my mother to stay back away from the window, just in case. No point in her surviving my news only to get shot by a stray bullet from the streets.

The next morning something really amazing happened. My mom and I went down to El Yaque Beach together. Ever since I was a young girl, my mother never really went into the water. I'd watch her, tall and extremely beautiful with flawless skin, and her dark, sculpted, perfect face, step into the water, with her hair pulled back, moving slowly but with effortless determination as she stepped in to where her ankles would be wet. Then she'd bend down and splash water on her face and her arms. She looked and moved with drama, like a work of art. She was graceful about the way she did it. I never thought anything of the way my mom behaved at the beach my entire life. That's just what my mom did at the beach as far back as I could remember. I have tons of pictures of my mom splashing water on her face but none of her actually in the water. She never went in past her feet. We spent a lot of time at the beach growing up too.

So that morning my mom took a small glass of whiskey with her down to the beach, just a little whiskey, maybe a shot. She was not a drinker; very rarely have I seen her drink. I didn't think a lot of it, but I was a little bit curious. The glass had a little safeguard on it so it wouldn't spill, like a child's sippy cup.

We were on a bay and the water was very shallow. We set down our things on the sand, and then something very strange happened. My mom walked into the bay with her little glass of whiskey and actually sat down in the shallow water. There she was, sitting down in the water with her whiskey glass, swirling the cup around. There were some kids splashing around nearby and people enjoying the beach like they would on any other day, and while I didn't immediately know why, something extraordinary was happening. I didn't ask any questions; I just joined her and sat down in the water too. I'd never seen her sit down in water before, ever.

She proceeded to tell me a story.

"Patricia, when I was young and I lived in the Indian village, there was a little river called Cañito. In order for us to go from one side of the river to the other side, we had to take a boat," she said.

"One morning, I was with your uncle and an older woman, and we had to cross the river, but there were no boats. There were eight young military men trying to find the boats to take people across. It was really, really hot in the village.

"So these eight men, thinking it was so hot and they could cool off, decide to swim to the other side to bring the boats back to get us."

My mom is a woman of few words, really. So as I sat there I marveled to hear a story of her childhood. As far as I knew, she'd never told any of us about this, or about anything from her childhood, ever. So I was somewhat captivated, listening to this and also still amazed, of course, that she was in the water.

"I was just five years old. I watched eight men go in to get the boats, but only five came back," she said. "Three were drowned by the seaweed. They got caught and couldn't get out."

As a little girl, she had to watch them pull the bodies of these young men out of the river that day, and from that moment on, she had been terrified of the water. So my mom told me this as she was in the water drinking her whiskey. I had tears in my eyes because I realized it had taken a lot for her to share this. She told me she'd never told the story to anyone before. I guarantee that my uncle had never told that story to my cousins either. My mom had been terrified of water all this time, and she never told anyone for fifty-something years until that moment. Even years before, she went out on that yacht that day with me but didn't want to tell me then she was afraid of water. Instead she had a severe panic attack.

I realized then, sitting in the water with her, that it had taken me telling my mom I was gay for her to be able to go in the water and say something about her life. It was at that moment that I understood by not saying who we want to be or who we really are, we are hurting other people. It was almost as if not sharing would have been selfish of me. The fact that I told my mom I was gay allowed her to tell me her biggest fear in life. Not even that day on the yacht, when she was obviously terrified, did she feel she could share this secret. But my bravery gave her courage.

After that she went into the water more often—never too deep, but she would get wet. But something else happened too. That morning in the water was the beginning of a new relationship with my mom, and I sort of became her confidante. It took one of us being open to start a new world of communication between us, and coming from an indigenous community, that's significant.

When you grow up indigenous, you don't really express yourself. It simply isn't done. We are very shy by nature, very withdrawn. There are so many cultures like that, especially for women, where discovering and revealing truth are frowned upon—the Latin community as well as many other cultures and religions. Women are taught not to express themselves, but also to take up little space and blend in to the background.

After I opened up to my mother, we started being more expressive, even hugging, which we hadn't really done. My sisters too.

Telling Fernando and my father—that was a different reaction altogether. Right after I told my mother, I went to Maracaibo to have lunch with my father at a local restaurant.

"Papá, remember that report in the paper that said I was dating a woman? Well, it's true. I am gay," I said before we even ordered.

"That's temporary. That's temporary," he said, almost pretending I hadn't said anything at all.

"No, Papá, I'm gay. I'm sorry I lied."

"That's temporary," he insisted, barely looking me in the eye as he spoke.

That was it. We didn't talk about it anymore. We just went on with our lunch, leaving the chill in the air. That ever-so-slight chill lasted for a long time, and, worse, he continued to make references to gay people that were negative—in jokes or whatever. My dad, and much of Latin culture, had done a lot of that over the years. But considering it was hurtful to me, I had hoped he would stop. I accepted it for years until I finally told him, "Papã, you can't keep doing this, because you're insulting me. You're insulting your daughter." He didn't respond, and we never discussed my sexuality again. On the upside, he's always been totally accepting and even sometimes asks about my girlfriends. Words, however, were never needed again. My dad, like any parent, did the best he could on all fronts. It took him time, but he got there.

Fernando was a little more disappointing and upset. When I finally told him I was gay, it didn't go well at all. When I told him, just after the conversation with my dad, he got angry, angry, angry and said, "Oh, no wonder you've been helping Mamã so much. It's because you felt guilty all those years. That's why you helped."

The pain of that statement cut deep. The actions that followed were devastating. After that very short conversation, he went an entire year without speaking to me. Not a word. I was in a lot of pain. I spoke to Mary often, and while Fernando wouldn't speak to me, Mary said he was in pain too. We had been very close. Mary suggested I write him a letter. So I did, from the heart. I acknowledged how difficult it must have been for him. I told him it was hard for me too, but I was who I was. I assured him what I did for my mother was out of love. Mostly, I wanted my brother back. I missed him, and I said that.

If not for Mary, who worked diligently behind the scenes to get him to accept me, we may never have spoken again. But finally we did. I went home for the holidays. Somehow, he just let it go, first by smiling; then, eventually, little by little, we picked up where we left off. For a short time afterward, something still lingered in the air, but we worked at it until finally one day he became my biggest ally once again. The lesson I learned is that everyone wouldn't react like my mother had. I needed time to process my truth, and Fernando needed his time to process his. My dad too. We put everything on the table, gave it time, and eventually love prevailed.

Chapter Twenty-Nine

By my second year dating Lisa, our differences began to make themselves apparent. Despite the fact that we loved each other, it became clear that we belonged to different worlds. I started missing home and my culture. I resented having to spend so much time in London, and the city started to feel very foreign to me. The jokes stopped being funny, and the travel was getting me down. Plus, I was never going to move there, and she was so successful at her work that she was never going to move to New York. One weekend we were in Ibiza, and Lisa left for home early while I stayed back with my Spanish friends. Everything just clicked once she had gone. I was with Gonzalo and other friends who felt like family, and I felt comforted by them. I wondered if Lisa had been feeling our differences as well. I called her from the airport the next morning. It was sad, but when we spoke it was clear to us both that it was time to end our relationship.

Around that time, I was getting into *Vogue*, *Cosmopolitan*, and *Marie Claire*, but those covers were not coming my way still—not in the United States. I had recently done a campaign for CoverGirl for the Hispanic market, and my agent, Glena, received a call from L'Oréal. They were interested in talking to me about doing a campaign. Around the same time, CoverGirl called. Glena and I went into a meeting at Grey Advertising in New York with a woman named Anne Martin-Vachon from CoverGirl. The entire team from CoverGirl was there, plus Jerry Saviola from Grey.

Katie came to the meeting too. That's how I knew it must have been big.

We all sat down in a conference room together to talk about why we were there.

"How would you feel about being the face of CoverGirl?" Jerry asked.

I thought that made sense since I was connecting with the Hispanic market. I wasn't overly excited initially until it became clear they weren't talking about the Latin market.

"You could be one of the faces of CoverGirl in the United States," said Jerry.

A Latina? Being the face of CoverGirl in the United States? Mainstream America?

It was shocking. I sat there trying to process what that really meant. For me. For Latina women. It meant we were an entity almost on our own. Not being grouped in with other ethnicities, but standing up as a people and being noticed for our look. The move would give us all a face in fashion. In Hollywood, it was around the same time Salma Hayek was making inroads in movies. There was a time in the not-too-distant past, and maybe it never went away, when Latinas played either whores or housekeepers on TV and in the movies. That was what we were. In fashion, we were big, dark, curvy girls. CoverGirl was about to redefine that, and I was going to be a part of it. We were going to expand the boundaries of beauty in the United States.

The challenge was that CoverGirl and L'Oréal were both talking to me at the same time, but I could only engage in a contract with one of them. Both were huge and meaningful to my career.

"Why don't we do something for Hispanic people as part of this deal?" I said.

"What exactly are you thinking?" asked Anne.

I had recently given some thought to the idea of giving back somehow— of doing something good for people who needed help. I'd watched Katie give back over the years and do so much work for human trafficking victims. It seemed easy to make that kind of contribution. "Well, education. My parents were both in education. We should do some kind of joint program to help the Hispanic education system." That seemed the obvious choice. The root of all sorts of problems was a lack of education. If we could educate more people, there would be less chaos in the world.

"Give us some time to explore the options. We like the idea—we just need to do our research."

We liked that they wanted to explore some options and that some good would come out of my contract with them. I went with CoverGirl. Seven months later they had developed a scholarship program, after learning through research that, at the time, 26 percent of Hispanic women did not finish high school, compared to 6 percent of Caucasian women and 13 percent of African-American women. The program was called the My Colors of Success initiative. It was an essay contest requesting that entrants write about embracing inner beauty and heritage and how it would help them succeed. Once it launched, I visited schools of very low-income families. A lot of firsts came from that deal with CoverGirl. I became the first Latina woman to become the face of CoverGirl in the US market. It was one of the first big American companies to take that kind of chance on a Latin person. It was the first time I worked with Anne at CoverGirl, a wonderful woman who later went on to take a lead role at HSN and with whom I reconnected many years later. It was my first exposure to seeing that a difference could be made, sparking my interest in starting the Wayuu Taya Foundation to help indigenous women and children in South America.

What was made most apparent by that experience was the lesson that businesses that promote sustainability and help communities can also be extremely successful in their core business—the two aren't separate goals. A company or individual doesn't have to wait to build something big and then donate money later—these things could be done side by side, and success is still attainable. I learned that through Russell Simmons, who made money and did good simultaneously, both working in and helping the community. That notion was very American to me, very New York.

Chapter Thirty

There was one incident in my life that filled me with such incomprehensible regret, I'm not sure I ever recovered.

Once the Wayuu Taya Foundation was up and running, I was making many trips to Venezuela for it. My cousin Maria Alexandra had prompted me to consider working with the Wayuu people after her father (my uncle), who helped my mother greatly, told Maria Alexandra on his deathbed not to forget the Wayuu people. On one visit in particular around 2004, I was holding a press conference to promote a cable company I did some work for called Inter. My Venezuelan manager of many years, Jesica Vivas, set up everything for me that took place at home, including this event. I hadn't spoken much to Jorge since I last visited his office. During this press conference, I stepped up to the podium, and there he was in the crowd. He looked tired. He was sitting up front with all the journalists, and seeing him made me shake. He'd had an accident and was in a wheelchair. He had gained weight. I muddled through the conference, distracted by his presence. Afterward we went into a room and spoke. He was sweet. I loved the man, regardless of my anger toward him for getting sick. He didn't look good. I was worried about his health, but I didn't show it properly.

"Jorge, how could this have happened?"

He said nothing. He had been humiliated enough. I didn't need to make it worse.

"I can't walk. I need a hip replacement," he said.

I loved him so much, but still I judged him.

"It's ten thousand dollars. Can you give it to me?" he asked.

I should have had the money, but I didn't have it on hand. The reality was I had invested in a beauty company I was trying to start and over time lost all my savings on the wrong decisions. I could, however, have gotten it for him through a loan or taken it from a credit card. Over all those years, after he gave me my start, he had never once asked me for anything.

"I don't have the money right now. But let me see what I can do."

I intentionally kept the conversation brief, my discomfort overtaking my sense of compassion.

I'll never know if he believed me or not, or if I was even telling myself the truth. But I left Jorge that day to travel to England. Simply put: Jorge's surgery wasn't a priority to me. I took my time and talked it over with a few people who said it wasn't for me to pay, that I didn't owe him anything. They were wrong. I was wrong for putting off my decision.

I should have listened to my heart. Jorge died not too long after that meeting. I never got the chance to do what was right, to do something for him—the man who gave me the opportunity of a lifetime and my career. When I heard the news, it was an enormous shock—like a punch in the gut that just never dissipated. It became the single biggest regret of my entire life. I didn't listen to my heart. Instead I let the burden of being needed take over. Jorge would have died eventually anyway, but he would have at least done it walking and knowing I cared about him. It was just a hip replacement, and I could have given him some pleasant remaining months.

That episode marked me. It taught me that it's impossible to go back in time and made me realize the importance of being present. Jorge was the first person I knew who was close and young who died. Moreover, the blame for his death fell squarely at my feet. He probably died disappointed in me. He had supported me when I revealed I was gay. He was the first gay person I'd ever met.

Venezuela became my next target for my compassion. The harsh realities of the people, the disadvantaged—we can't just live in those realities only when we are in the midst of them. We have to work not to forget, and not to let others forget. Time passes too quickly and doesn't stop while the rest of us figure out the difference between right and wrong.

Chapter Thirty-One

After breaking up with Lisa, I once made love in three time zones, in three cities, to three different women in one day. Flying west made that possible, or it certainly helped anyway. I casually dated a lot of women that year. Maybe there was some need to experiment or something, because that sort of behavior wasn't exactly in my soul. It was possible I was suppressing my feelings by using women to numb my pain. I kept relationships short and uncomplicated. It was almost as if I'd anticipated my life coming to this lonely point; and then when it did, it didn't hurt so much because I had prepared myself. It was crushes only, never getting too attached to anyone.

There was one woman that year I did care for deeply, who could have been serious, but she wasn't up for the life of being a gay woman. I judged her for not having strength to live that life, which was ironic considering that, in my not-too-distant past, that strength to come clean had eluded me too.

Around that same time, I started making inroads in Hollywood. I'd hit all the high watermarks in modeling—*Sports Illustrated Swimsuit Edition*, *Victoria's Secret*, and every fashion magazine and designer out there. Studying acting had become my passion. I'd landed a recurring role on *Arrested Development* and had some parts in shows such as *CSI*, *American Family,* and others. While I traveled back and forth between coasts, I started to yearn for a relationship and some stability.

My friend Michelle had been telling me about a woman named Lauren whom I needed to meet. She arranged a group dinner at the Mercer Hotel in New York one night and invited Lauren. I was immediately struck by how much we looked alike and, after speaking with her only briefly, how culturally similar we were. Her parents were from Mexico, which is where I grew up. She was born in the United States and lived in LA. We started a fling in New York, but nothing came of it because we felt too similar. Plus, the timing was off for us. A year went by and we remained friends. I had to travel to Mexico for a shoot with *American Family*. I called her from there.

"It's my birthday this week," I told her.

"I know. What are you doing for your birthday?" she asked.

"Working, I guess."

She must have been able to tell from my voice that I had no plans. "Why don't I come down? It's a quick flight. We'll hang out," she said.

I was floored. Lauren hopped on a flight a few days later and joined me. It was meant to be just as friends, but the gesture touched me deeply. She joined us for a crew dinner the night she arrived. I sat there staring at her during the meal. All of a sudden I saw her. Her smile and laughter captivated me immediately. She wasn't the person I was with in New York. She was suddenly family to me, rooted in her culture. I felt she had to be my girlfriend. That night, we made love in the most effortless way I'd ever made love with anyone. It was tender, soft, giving, and easy. I fell madly in love.

When Lauren left Mexico I missed her terribly. Once we wrapped, instead of driving from the desert in Mexico to San Diego to catch a plane to New York, I had the production driver take me nine hours to her house in LA so we could have dinner. That night I flew to New York, knowing I was simply picking up my things and turning around and heading back to LA to move in with this woman. It was that clear.

Lauren was different from anyone I'd dated. She made me want to be better at relationships. She was Latina, so she was close to my culture. She was a stable Virgo, which helped too. She made me want to try for love. That's not to say she hadn't shown some resistance; she was worried it was too soon. I wasn't.

Because it had all happened so quickly, we'd never really taken the time to have a serious conversation about the future. When we finally did, I was confronted with a situation I'd encountered before.

"Patricia," she said, within a few months of my arrival there, "I've always wanted to have a baby. So you need to know that I'm going to have one. If that's something you don't want, then it's better if you don't stay for too long."

Cravings of something solid had stirred up inside of me. It wasn't so much kids that were in my head, but the idea of family—my own family—was appealing.

"Why not," I said. "Let's do it."

My words weren't convincing. She didn't seem excited to hear them. No smile, no plan to get started.

"What's wrong?" I asked.

"Well, you travel so much. I know your life is fueled by work, and your work is generated by travel. I'm never going to tell you not to do it, but it's going to be difficult for us to raise a child together if you're gone all the time."

"We'll work on that, then," I said, not certain I was sincere about changing my habits and staying in one place. But I rented out my apartment in New York on Jane Street and gave it my best shot full time in LA.

It was tough going at first.

I'd never been with anyone in the corporate world. Lauren would leave for work in the morning, and I'd be there in this house in the hills trying to generate some work that wouldn't require travel. I missed New York, of course. Los Angeles, where we lived, had too much nature. Some days I felt suffocated by the silence, almost like I couldn't breathe. It bothered me that Lauren left every morning. It was almost a feeling of abandonment, not being her priority.

I went crazy, getting controlling, irritated, and jealous for no good reason. I had never behaved like that before.

"What's wrong with you?" she'd ask some days when she arrived home and I'd lay into her immediately. I wanted all of her time. I didn't want her friends having any of it. Then I'd start in on her about making me move from New York, then about her working too long. Suddenly she had to be responsible for my happiness. She tried to manage me and take my fits in stride, but being with me in those early days must have been unbearable.

One evening, I don't even remember what I started in on her about, but I pushed her so far, she kicked the oven. Later that night, we had plans out, and we got into another argument based on a comment I'd made about a mutual friend. She was so angry that she hit the wall. I'd bought her a ring, and she had used the hand she wore it on to hit the wall. The ring got bent. I'd picked a fight again.

Later that night she said, "I can't do this anymore. You don't trust me, and I can't be responsible for your happiness." This led to us ending the relationship almost as quickly as it had begun. It was even more heartbreaking because it was New Year's Eve and I was going to be alone.

I flew home to Margarita Island to a house I had bought just before meeting Lauren. I'd always wanted a home there, and when I had the money my mom went and found one for me. It was a place I loved that had become the center of my life, not only because of the location, but because I'd met a neighbor named Evelyn who grew to become one of the dearest people in my world. At the hands of my mother, I'd been connected to my sacred place and a woman who helped me understand and believe in my inner strength.

When I arrived there after three connections and eighteen hours, I walked directly up to one of the giant round wooden pillars that led up to the door. I wrapped my arms around one of them and held on tightly. I hugged it. It was my house. My home. My sanity. My center. My soul. I sobbed. I had been so far away from myself. I had betrayed myself so many times in my life, and this time I'd given away my power. Things needed to change. I needed to be with Lauren, that was clear, but in a healthy way. If she would take me back.

I called Lauren that night, and we talked. She told me I needed to change and work on myself. I agreed to do just that, and I planned on going on a spiritual retreat at the Landmark Forum for a few days. I told her we needed to move into the city, or closer at least. We needed a house that was ours. She agreed. And she said something else profound.

"There's something you need to know about me. I always try my best. I always do the best I can."

Those words just clicked. I thought, *This woman truly loves me.* I hadn't understood it until that moment. I had trained myself to think the worst, but the best was sitting right in front of me. She came home at 8:00 at night, sure, but she came home. She came home to me. In return I tortured her. Life changed after that because I finally realized love was possible. Being loved was okay, not just for other people, but for me too. I flashed back to my life growing up. My dad did his best; I just never saw it because I wasn't looking. I saw poverty and lack of food and a struggling mother. But he did his best. Lauren's words were eye-opening and liberating. In an instant I understood why I had tortured myself for a lifetime, never trusting anyone enough to tell them my secret. I didn't know we were all just doing our best. We were all just trying to get by.

Had I understood that and trusted love, maybe I would have saved us all a lot of grief.

Gay marriage wasn't legal when Lauren and I decided to commit to one another and have a baby together. The decision was an easy one, not like when it had been presented to me before. It made sense. Lauren was an amazing woman, and I was excited to bring a life into the world with her.

The second we received confirmation she was pregnant, I felt like my entire life changed for the better. Then this tiny bundle of a baby came into the world, and my heart swelled in ways that I couldn't ever put into words. Maya was born and true joy filled my world. Everything suddenly made sense. Every ounce of heartbreak, every moment of joy, all that I'd struggled for—it no longer mattered. The lying and the truth—now each event was part of a whole, an entirety that paved the path to the place where I was meant to arrive. I walked my journey as I was supposed to walk it, and it led me to the most utterly profound love of all: the love for our child, Maya, the greatest love and joy of my life.

Epilogue

Despite all my movies, TV, and modeling work, my favorite project was for the Public Theater in New York City with Philip Seymour Hoffman. We were performing *School of the Americas* with the Labyrinth Company. The Public Theater is an amazing place of art and equality, where every actor wants to return to work regardless of their fame. What worried me, having never done anything of this significance or caliber, was performing two shows a day. That seemed utterly daunting. I prepared with diligence, taking it very seriously as I did all my work.

Once we finished rehearsals, I decided it would be smart of me to hold back somewhat in the first performance on opening day and then give it my all in the second show of the day. I intended to do the matinee with just a little less of myself, saving something for later. That way, by the evening show, I'd be energized and ready to run with it. During the first performance, I went out there and did what I had planned. It felt like the right approach—I felt like I had energy left, and therefore the second show would be great. I did the second show, but it was a disaster. I never got where I needed to get with my performance. It was simply awful. The reaction from my fellow actors onstage was muted as a result of my performances, and the audience's energy in response to my delivery was diluted. Everything felt flat. I left the stage knowing I'd blown it and dragged the cast down with me. Instead of my performance in one show being good and the second being great, both were terrible. Dejected, I made my way up the dark stairs to the dressing room. Philip was sitting there on the couch on the landing, lights off, as I knew he would be. He could likely see the pain on my face, that I knew it hadn't gone well. I stopped, and before he could say anything, I apologized for messing up.

"I feel terrible. I've disappointed you," I said. "I'm so sorry."

He paused for a second to gather his thoughts and looked at me with his comforting eyes. "Patricia," he said, "an actor should never hold back. Not for a rehearsal, not for a performance. The harder you push, the further you will go. You'll go places that you never knew existed—beyond where you ever expected you could get if you pushed your hardest." I gave him a hug that night and never held back again on that stage, or in anything else I performed, after that.

He taught me so much during that show, but those words about not holding back resonated beyond the stage too. In my lifetime I've spent a lot of time feeling sad. It seems to be my comfort zone. It might have to do with being an actress but also likely my heritage. We're fighters and survivors, not victims, but we have it in our blood to be submissive. There's an element of being an underdog as well. Sometimes I slide back into that role ever so slightly before climbing back out and remembering we're not living a dress rehearsal. There's no room to hold back. Some people say the days are long. I say the days are short. Time moves too quickly to save something for later. That's not to say knowing that makes life easy. It's not easy at all on the best of days. It takes work. But the awareness of all that helps.

Intense travel was and will likely always be a part of my life, and that took a toll on my relationship with Lauren. In LA things were great, but when a trip came along, it was always tense for us. Communication was never our strong suit either, despite how much we loved each other. After being together for eight years, Lauren and I broke up, but we maintained joint custody of Maya. Once we decided it was over, I spent a month slowly moving my things into my new apartment nearby. But I rented all the furniture—I wasn't prepared to commit to a couch. I knew it would take a while to order, and it was already so upsetting that I didn't want to move into a bare apartment; I thought it would make me feel worse. But by the time I spent my first night there, well, it couldn't have been any more painful for me. I had painted the place first before I moved in, and I was actually feeling a little bit excited about it all. I was creating a second home for Maya, and I wanted her to feel as safe and happy in it as she did in her other home. I decorated her room purple and pink. Part of the reason I'd taken my time getting there was so that it wouldn't be so abrupt for Maya. I thought if she had this really great room, that might help too. We didn't want to tell Maya I was leaving and then the next day just not be there. So we took some time with it, using that month to ease her into it. I left for good during the day while she was at school. I thought that would make it easier for her. It might have; I hope it did. But for me, I discovered nothing made it easier or prepared me for what it would feel like that first night.

I was lying in bed alone for the first time in years without Maya under the same roof as me. The rental furniture made it worse. I was there in a rented bed, and I felt really, really lost because I knew right then that Maya was my child, but it was different from being a regular mom. It had always been a concern in the back of my mind, an issue for me, but until that moment, that night, it hadn't been real. That night it was too real, and it hurt. It killed me. I didn't close my eyes for even one second. I might have lain there for several nights, or weeks even, had my dear friend Evelyn not surprised me with a visit to help me get moving. She showed up with a blue chair and red table for Maya. The gesture was a rescue and a reminder of her true essence as a person.

Maya is my child by love, and of course legally. She has the spirit of both Lauren and me, and she shares many traits with me, including my love of language. Even though she's blonde, she even looks like me. But Lauren will always be—and I respect this 100 percent—her first mommy. She carried her. And I will be her second mommy. I realized this that night. I guess I always sort of knew this, but not in such a stark way. When we made decisions, I'd been careful to respect Lauren. I never took Maya with me when I traveled, though I really would have loved to, because it wouldn't have been fair. It was a huge struggle, and I lost a lot of work because I wanted to be near Maya. Being away was too disruptive for her.

Despite the pain of not being with Maya, something amazing and unexpected emerged following my breakup with Lauren: our relationship as a couple ended, but our love grew. It became a different kind of love. We are more of a family now than we ever could have imagined. Breaking up wasn't a failure. The relationship was a victory because the most important thing happened: we had a child together. Splitting up had always been so tragic for me in the past, but while it all hurt with Lauren, my life didn't get depleted except that I missed being with Maya all the time.

My life with Lauren became richer in the years after we separated. Our love was no longer romantic, but it was bigger than that. It all turned out okay, and that was an amazing and unexpected result for us all. So much so that Lauren encouraged me to start dating online, which we found funny when we really thought about it from a practical standpoint, because I couldn't even post a picture or describe what I did for a living because of my celebrity.

Not being with Maya does hurt, but we're all going to be okay. The hard part is that Maya has always felt the pain over the separation differently from how a child might have felt if her father had left. If I were straight, I'd have been the number one mommy and my child would have been with me on location when I traveled. I say this knowing there is no way around it, but it is painful, even years later. It's just different, the relationship between a mother and daughter, and Maya feels for me as her mother, so when one of her mothers is gone, it's agonizing. She recently said it's "too hard having two mommies." I struggle with my situation now because I don't live with Maya full time, and I travel often, like a father would, but I am a mother. My child feels the absence of a mother, and I miss her because I *am* her mother. The emotions I'm experiencing in the wake of the separation are universal among mothers, gay and straight, but the realities of the situation are cruelly and painfully unique.

I remember my mother telling me once, when she saw us together—Lauren, Maya, and me—that I was living a borrowed life. Those words rang true that night in my new apartment, and I've tried to be aware of that tendency since. I had borrowed this life, and then all of a sudden I had to give it back. The hole it left in my heart, giving it back, was irreparable. I didn't expect that pain. You don't know it until you know it. I frequently borrowed people's lives. Lauren's wasn't the first one.

We can't really change our reality, but we can figure out how to live our own lives. I tried to give Maya a brother or sister on my own for two years. Like so many women who struggle to get pregnant, I did natural insemination, the fertility treatments—shots, pills, hormones, and then in vitro—but to no avail. I was able to get pregnant but unable to carry the baby. The combination of being away from Maya and the realization that I was unable to bring another child into the world for her simply gutted me. Between Christmas and New Year's Eve in 2013, I was feeling extremely low. It was almost as painful as that first night away from Maya. Everything had all spiraled downward into an inconsolable sadness. Numbness had washed over me, and something had cracked through the shell I'd built around my heart to hide my sadness over being away from my child for the holidays, perhaps, and then not being able to give her a sibling. Sometimes my heart breaks from the consequences of my choices. This week in particular hurt badly. I was considering for the first time in my life taking medication to get out of the slump. The doctor diagnosed me with depression. I could barely get off the couch. My friend Alfonso from Dallas was in town at the time. He called and told me I should meet his friend Lekha. He was insistent. I agreed to invite her to yoga. New Year's Eve day, I forced myself to get up, get dressed, and go to class, mostly because I felt oddly drawn to meeting this woman. It was the only reason I got up. Looking back at how blue I felt, I'm surprised I was able to move, but I did. I went to Russell's yoga studio in LA, Hot 8 Yoga.

I'd been crying in the car before I went into class. I pulled myself together and found Lekha in the lobby. We introduced ourselves and went into class. World music was playing softly when we walked into the studio. I could smell eucalyptus from the steam lightly coming down from the ceiling. The heat was intense, but not like the very hot yoga rooms. I put down my mat, closed my eyes, and held back tears before we began. Lekha was Indian. She was tall and had beautiful long, curly hair. I immediate felt her presence and sense of calm as she set up beside me. She didn't ask any questions, but she could see that I was sad, so she reached out and held my hand. Her gesture made me feel compassion toward myself maybe for the first time. That's something we never really consider, that we all show compassion toward other people but rarely show it toward ourselves. I gave myself a break in that moment, realizing it was okay to feel broken or defeated, that I wasn't perfect. None of us is perfect. We can't give our children everything, and we can't give ourselves everything. We can just do our best and give ourselves the same level of compassion we extend to others. It was an epiphany: that morning led to my decision to stop trying to get pregnant and the acceptance that it was okay. There was a collective energy—like all the stars aligned—in Lekha's spirit, the yoga room's energy, the end and beginning of a new year. It all contributed to the change. I had to hit the low in the days leading up to that class to find the high. That came from within me. By the time I left yoga that morning, my head was clear and I felt light. My sadness and loneliness evaporated. I felt ready for what was before me, but mostly I felt peace.

I have learned so much from all my life experiences—good and bad—and I wouldn't trade even the lows for anything. I am stronger and better for having walked through them all. Kabbalah has helped me with that. Kabbalah teaches you to take responsibility for your actions. It's about taking action. It teaches us that the universe will never give us anything we can't handle. I learned from my mistakes over the years, overcame a lot of anguish, kicked down many doors, but ultimately it was my truth that set me free. My life feels authentic and unburdened now. My openness became my true joy and gave me a second chance to find peace, love, and real freedom, and it gave me the opportunity to spread it around to those I love.

People have asked me: Why now? Why keep my sexuality a secret from the public all those years and then suddenly feel the urge to tell the world? The fashion world, which is all about being fresh and unique and creative, was of course very open and accepting of the gay community even decades ago, but the irony of being an international beauty and symbol of femininity has never been lost on me. Once I started acting, I remained quiet to protect my craft. There was *Celebrity Apprentice* too, and we all know how much Donald Trump loves a pretty woman. Hollywood actors and actresses have a right to share to whatever extent they choose. They have to portray many different faces in a career, and sometimes that means not letting the public in on much about them, which is a challenge for superstars. I respect those who keep it to themselves and urge them to continue if they need to.

Revealing my secret to my inner circle unexpectedly changed something else within me. Before I came out, I used to hide my sexiness unless I was being paid to flaunt it. I felt ashamed of it and confused by it, maybe because I was living a lie. My sexy side was only for hire as a model. This notion made it feel ugly to me, and I worked hard to cover it up whenever possible. Looking back, it was an effort to prove to the other side of my world that I was, in fact, gay. But once I told the truth and had nothing to prove to anyone, I unleashed an ability to own my looks and own my beauty. Once I was honest about being gay, I was honest about enjoying being sexy. I was able to accept that everyone who was gay didn't also have to maintain a masculine status, though at times there's a big, butch dyke in me, not just a lipstick lesbian. Now we can embrace our feminine and masculine side, and that's okay. Gay women are beautiful, so with nothing to prove to myself or anyone else, I felt free just to be. I love men for their ability to be honest with their desires. Knowing that, now I allow myself to enjoy my femininity as well. Heels and skirts are no longer for work only. The truth gave me choice. The truth unlocked confidence.

It unlocked a new world for me professionally as well. I learned I am not all glitz and glam and legs. I have a strong head for business as well. I helped create a very successful hair care company called Taya Beauty, producing products whose key ingredients come from programs that are sustainable, organic, and environmentally friendly from indigenous communities in the Amazon. It wasn't easy getting this company off the ground. My first attempt at starting a company left me broke and disillusioned. I had made one big mistake in getting started, but it was a mistake that turned into a lesson for me. Once I realized what had gone wrong, I was forced to make a decision: fight and perpetuate a misstep, or trust my gut and walk away from a massive emotional and financial investment. I walked away. I dug deep from within, knowing I had it in me to rebuild. The universe and my faith told me all would be okay. It was a life-changing decision because it taught me a lot about myself. Plus, I lost everything. Everything I had went into that company. My resolve and self-confidence told me if I built it once, I could build it again. Today Taya Beauty is sold worldwide and is one of HSN's top hair care brands.

I also started a charitable foundation, The Wayuu Taya Foundation, which has a tremendous impact on the lives of the indigenous people of Latin America. Evelyn was such a positive force in getting the foundation up and running. I thought small; she thought big. She pushed me to do more than I imagined possible. The foundation feeds and educates hundreds of children and empowers women through sustainable projects to better their lives and communities. At the same time, my work invigorates the spirit of a crowd of influential, affluent good friends in New York eager to join in my efforts, to donate, and to be part of the circle that supports my work.

It's important to start a dialogue between women everywhere in every culture—gay or straight—that encourages them to be open and empowered. I urge women of all cultures, not just Latin ones: Be seen. Be heard. It is especially important in Venezuela, where discussions about religion, politics, or family have been quieted. It saddens me deeply to see how my country has deteriorated on all fronts. The strife of the people there is unimaginable. I hope to inspire people there and everywhere to be proud and to shout their feelings from the rooftops. I believe, through my spiritual following of Kabbalah, that speaking up heals not only the person doing the talking, but also the person doing the listening. I feel hiding secrets hurts, not helps, and that sometimes trying to shield other people from the pain of the truth is a huge disservice to them. Truth frees people to experience their journey and process. I want to at least start a dialogue about being Latina and gay. The tide is changing. It's time to take action, specifically in the Latin communities, which have long avoided the topic.

There are many reasons I wrote this book, but primarily I wrote it for my daughter, Maya. I want Maya to be free to be who she wants to be and to live in a world free of prejudice and bias. If I can stand up and tell the world a secret I held for so long, and felt so much shame over for so many years, maybe that will give her the strength to live an honest, authentic life as well. I want my daughter to be truthful to her nature and to take pride in everything she does and is. It doesn't matter if someone is standing up to say they're gay or not; it boils down to being proud of whatever we do in our lives.

Acknowledgments

I'm consistently wowed by the power and strength of women when we all work together and stand up for each other. In so many situations personally and professionally, I have witnessed women doing amazing things for other women. It's our responsibility to help each other. So many of you have given your time and energy to me in every industry, including the very personal process of writing this book. And, of course, some wonderful men helped too! I want to thank everyone who contributed to this memoir.

First, let me thank Stephanie Krikorian. Without you believing so strongly in this project, it never would have happened. It's because of your tireless commitment and zeal that *Straight Walk* finally saw the light of day. During the writing process, you had an excellent ability to identify which details of my life and journey were most important and would be most impactful, and worked masterfully to organize them on the page. Thanks for taking such care with my words and my personal experiences, which weren't always easy for me to dredge up. This started as a writing project but quickly turned into a friendship that I greatly cherish. I can't wait to find something else for us to work on together.

My sincerest thanks to the entire team at Post Hill Press for making this book a reality. Your enthusiasm for the project from the start has been so encouraging.

My editor, Lara Asher, gave this book an intense amount of love and attention. Simply put: she made it better than I could have imagined.

Thank you for your keen eye. Diana Nuhn did an amazing job creating a cover I'm proud to have hold together the pages of my story. Thank you. Thank you Meredith Litt Dias for your meticulous copy edits.

What many people don't realize is that with any book or movie or work of art, there are people behind the scenes making sure the wheels keep turning and the contracts get created and signed. For me, that team not only provides great expertise, but offers much appreciated friendship and support as well. Thank you, Ivan De Paz, Marcia Daley, Cris Armenta, Hannah Roth, Eliot Lebenhart, Glena Marshall, Robert Goldstone, David Wilson, and Jesica Vivas for your help both over the years and in the future.

To my dear friends Lisa Gorman and Gonzalo Garcia, who made immense contributions to this project, helping me fill in the blanks in my history. Thank you for enthusiastically contributing to the book, and for at times having a better memory than I do. There were many early readers who offered guidance and wisdom, and who reviewed each word with care. They are Romer Gonzalez, Laura Semprun, Lekha Singh, Kat Cohen, and Natalie Fousekis. My heart is warmed because you were all so generous with your time.

There wouldn't be a book if there hadn't been a rewarding career to write about. There wouldn't be a career if a long list of women hadn't taken a chance and blind leap of faith on me. The opportunities I've gotten, on the runway and onstage, were paved with the heart and soul of some of the most tremendous women on this planet. I continue to be amazed by your contributions to business and the arts, and to the women you work with. I'm truly indebted to you, Katie Ford, Iris Minier, Ivana Chubbuck, Anne Martin-Vachon, Kathy Eldon, and Sheila Gray. You beautiful women could fuel the world with your charisma, smarts, integrity, and love.

We certainly met under the strangest of conditions, but our friendship has grown to mean the world to me. Thank you, Evelyn Brea, for knowing when I need you most even when I don't know myself.

Gabriela Nuñez, you are a reminder that we all have different friends for different reasons. There are so many reasons you are one of the most important people in my life, but the fact that you are home to me tops the list. Thanks for always being there.

To the tireless team at the Wayuu Taya Foundation: Bladimir Aguilera, Elainy Albornoz, Lisbeth Palma, Lulu Betancur, Camilla Olsson, Asmiria Roa, Asmiria Semprun, Vickyellen Rodriguez, Mayte Osorio, Sarah

Digby, Hector Rojas, Michelle Jean, Alexis Bracho, Pamela Landman, Osmaira Leon, Jesmary Manzi, Raiza Adinilda Cambar, Leilani Johnson, and Stephanie Marcantonio. You freed me up to write this book while holding ground at our charity, continuously dedicating your efforts to something that is so dear to us all.

The Taya Beauty team put up with my absence as well. Thanks for enduring the sleepless nights bouncing from Toronto to Munich and for talking me through ideas for this project. Thanks to Kenneth Browning, Luis Pascual, Julie Groome, and Arlene Ferro for giving it your all each day.

Jorge, there are simply not enough words to express my gratitude for all you have done. Out of respect for you, I've changed your name in this book. I hope your family reads this and knows this project is an homage— a tribute and a salute to you. I will remember you always.

Kevyn Aucoin, I hope you're up there kicking back with Jorge. Thanks for always being warm and present, and for making me feel welcome in an unfamiliar world. You and Eric Sakas were always so kind to me.

It was my Kabbalah teachers— Rabbi Philip Berg, Yehuda Berg, Karen Berg, Michal Berg, Michael Berg, Batsheva Zimerman, and Shalom Sharabi—who provided the foundation for me to write this book. The spiritual teaching of Kabbalah allowed me to turn every moment and every story into an authentic one that I humbly hope provides positivity to others.

Lauren Carr: I love you for bringing our daughter, Maya, into this world. My gratitude and love for you is infinite, more than a few sentences or any declaration I could make. You are family to me and always will be. More, you taught me to trust. I learned how to let go and trust through you. I'm honored to have you in my life.

Ileanna Simancas, you give me hope and unconditional love every day. I remember vividly that afternoon when you picked me up at the airport in Miami, when we were just friends of eleven years. You pulled up to the curb in your little light green Fiat, with Yordano playing. We were going to talk about our shared concerns over Venezuela, and then you put your hand on my leg and my world opened up to something new and precious. Thank you for so carefully reading each and every word of this book, putting up with my angst and my time away as I wrote it, and for sharing your heart, skill, and depth with me. I can't wait for many more years of love, perfectly packed suitcases, and laughter together.

As for my family, you are the best. I'm so blessed beyond words for being born into your worlds. Juan, Carlos, Fernando, Caty, and Limayri— you are cherished. I crave your laughter and smiles when I'm not with you. My sisters-in-law, Marisabel Ferreira, Elizabeth Moralez, Laura Gonzalez; my brothers-in-law, Felipe Estevez and Norman Watson; and all my nieces and nephews: Juan Carlos, Mario, Samuel, Ana Valeria, Isabel Cristina, Andres, Sofia, Valentina, Rudi, Nico, Wyatt, and Cody— thank you for enhancing every day with your affection. Also, to all my aunts, uncles, and cousins: I'm so happy to have all of you (and so many of you!) in my life. You are all home to me.

To my dad, Adalberto Velasquez: I love you and thank you for your commitment and dedication to our family. Thanks for teaching me about the world and inspiring me to learn more every day. I hope the words on these pages are half as good as everything you've ever written.

Of course, the two most impressive women in my life deserve all I have to give in this world: my mother, Lidela Semprun, whose sacrifices, hard work, and unconditional love made me who I am. You're inspiring as a woman and as a mother, and I thank you for all you provided me with in life. And my precious daughter, Maya: you are my world and my true joy. Watching you laugh and smile and grow is nothing short of a gift. I know you'll make a difference on this planet. I can't wait to see all that you accomplish with your amazing spirit and kindness. The three things I'm most grateful for: you, you, and you.

I could have filled one dozen pages naming people whose love and friendship has given me strength over the years and who enrich my life every day. Thank you all. But I can't list everyone, so thanks to a few of you who eased the stress of writing this book, and helped in some way with the story. Thank you for your support and love, Lorena Giavalisco, Erasmo Colon, Miguel Cardenas, Rafael Guzman (no longer with us), Gloria Salas, Martha Mijares, Lisa Ljung, Marco De La Cruz, Isabella Cascarano, Beatriz Vazquez, Linda Carbon, Margarita Cadenas, Juan Pacheco, Matt Cooper, Omar Hernandez, Rafael Del Carpio, Denisse Williams, Jose Mendoza, Sonja Nuttal, Yvo Hernandez, Jenny Woodman, Flor Salazar, Jacqueline Solis, Maria Ramirez, Alessandra Taddei, Alicia Garcia, Roger Vargas, Liz Mago, Sabine Manas, Vicky Steckel, Eloisa Maturen, Mimi Lazo, and my Liz in September family.